THE BOOK O
CRYSTAL
GRIDS

THE BOOK OF
CRYSTAL
GRIDS

A PRACTICAL GUIDE TO ACHIEVING YOUR DREAMS

PHILIP PERMUTT

CICO BOOKS

LONDON NEW YORK

Published in 2017 by CICO Books
An imprint of Ryland Peters & Small Ltd
20–21 Jockey's Fields   341 E 116th St
London WC1R 4BW   New York, NY 10029

www.rylandpeters.com

10 9 8 7

A CIP catalog record for this book is available from
the Library of Congress and the British Library.

ISBN: 978-1-78249-482-9

Printed in China

MIX
Paper from
responsible sources
FSC® C106563
www.fsc.org

Editor: Marion Paull
Designer: Louise Turpin
Illustrators: Trina Dalziel, Louise Turpin,
Cathy Brear, and Stephen Dew
Photographers: Roy Palmer and James Gardner
Stylists: Nel Haynes and Joanna Thornhill

Commissioning editor: Kristine Pidkameny
Senior editor: Carmel Edmonds
In-house designer: Fahema Khanam
Art director: Sally Powell
Production manager: Gordana Simakovic
Publishing manager: Penny Craig
Publisher: Cindy Richards

SAFETY NOTE

Please note that while the descriptions of the
properties of crystals refer to healing benefits, they
are not intended to replace diagnosis of illness or
ailments, or healing or medicine. Always consult
your doctor or other health professional in the
case of illness.

CONTENTS

INTRODUCTION

People globally have been working with crystals, gemstones, rocks, and minerals for thousands of years to promote health, happiness, and well-being. In this book, I refer to them all as crystals.

Crystals have been placed in powerful sacred configurations, alignments, and grids in many places and cultures around the world, such as the World Peace Crystal Grids placed at the North and South Poles, the breastplate of the biblical High Priest, Stonehenge and Avebury stone circles in Wiltshire, UK, and the Native American Indian Medicine Wheel/ Medicine Mountain National Historic Landmark in Wyoming, USA, to create centers of power and a focus of intention. They have been used to bring or enhance health, wealth, happiness, and lifestyle. They are regularly employed in the practise of feng shui as cures to many ills.

People across the world have a natural affinity with, and knowledge of, crystals and their amazing powers. Once you start collecting and working with crystals it is natural to begin arranging them in patterns. These patterns are subconscious crystal grids that reflect your unspoken desires, needs, and state of mind.

Our twenty-first-century technological lifestyle relies totally on crystals and some of their scientific applications, such as ruby crystals in laser technology or the latest advances in quartz-based memory in computing.

Crystal grids improve the quality of life by the application of crystals as tools for focusing energy, allowing the crystals to work together as a team, supporting each other to enhance every area of your life. This can bring many benefits, improving health, happiness, and prosperity. Although few people can see the energy directed through the crystal grid, it is possible that forces are being generated on sub-atomic levels through the zero-point field, which create these changes physically, emotionally, mentally, and spiritually.

Research into quantum physics has shown that distant healing with crystals does have an effect on patients.[1] It is also known that the energy of the person conducting and observing an experiment influences the outcome of that experiment. One of the most bizarre premises of

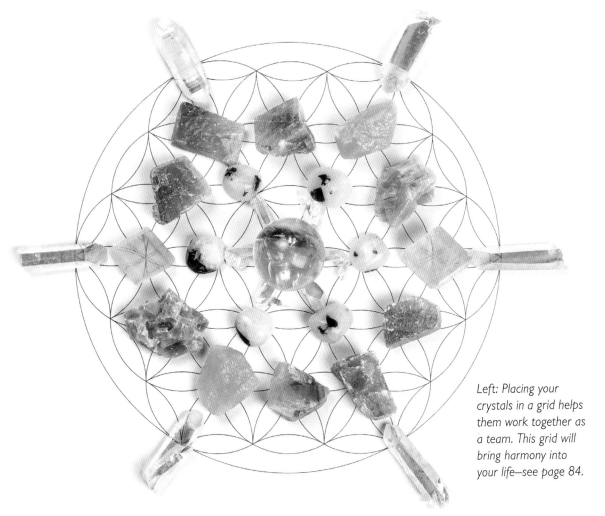

Left: Placing your crystals in a grid helps them work together as a team. This grid will bring harmony into your life—see page 84.

quantum theory, which has long fascinated philosophers and physicists alike, states that by the very act of watching, the observer affects the observed reality.[2] That means we can change reality by being there! So in creating a crystal grid, your focused intent adds to the crystals' effect.

Crystals are renowned throughout the world as natural healers. However, they not only heal, they also affect how we feel and our responses to the world around us. They are natural energy-boosters, helping to enhance our experience of living at every level, and can protect us by detoxifying our physical, emotional, and spiritual systems from the stresses and strains of twenty-first-century lifestyles. Within a crystal grid their potential is enhanced, magnified, and directed.

Crystal grids can work for anyone—adults and children, mothers and fathers, lovers and friends, engineers, business people, sales people, managers, directors, workers, and home makers. Crystal grids can help anyone.

CHAPTER 1

THE POWER OF CRYSTAL GRIDS

CRYSTAL HEALING

CRYSTAL THERAPY HAS LONG BEEN USED AS A GENTLE SYSTEM OF HOLISTIC HEALING. CRYSTALS ARE CREATED BY THE NATURAL ENERGIES OF THE PLANET AND WE CAN HARNESS THAT ENERGY TO HEAL OURSELVES PHYSICALLY, EMOTIONALLY, AND SPIRITUALLY.

Technically, "a crystal is a solid whose atoms are arranged in a highly ordered repeating pattern. These patterns are called crystal lattices. If an object has its atoms arranged in one of seven crystal lattice patterns, then that object is a crystal" (International Gem Society). However, when I write "crystal" in this book, I'm using the term colloquially to refer to the entire mineral kingdom—crystals, gemstones, rocks, stones, pebbles on a beach, giant megaliths, and minerals.

Crystals have an amazing natural power. They are the fundamental basis of twenty-first-century lifestyle, employed in many ways throughout technology, such as ruby crystals in red lasers (green lasers have alexandrite crystals and blue ones sapphire crystals). Another example is quartz or tourmaline crystals used to create a solid-state electric field in almost all modern electrical items. Put simply, without crystals we would be living very different lives without our computers, washing machines, or the international space station.

So we don't need to delve into the science of crystals in technology; it's all around us just about every minute of every day. What I'm interested in is how these amazing gifts of Mother Earth can help us in our daily lives and expand our conscious living.

Crystals have been worked with for millennia by people from all cultures around the world. They have adorned the pharaohs of ancient Egypt, bringing power and health, and the hippies of the sixties, helping to create a new level of awareness, shift in consciousness, and liberating freedoms throughout many countries. They live for millions of years. Some crystals are as ancient as the solid world—a few, such as zircon crystals from Australia, are two billion years old—and the ability of crystals to heal on many levels is unquestioned among their proponents. They give you the help you need to change what physically happens in your life.

HOLD ON! DID YOU JUST SAY THEY "LIVE" FOR MILLIONS OF YEARS?

Yes. Crystals are living beings! There are three kingdoms of living beings on planet earth—animals, plants, and minerals. Crystals live in geological time, not human time, so their life span is millions of years! Let me explain ... since the

Below: Ancient stones— zircon crystals from Australia can be up to two billion years old.

1970s, when I was in university studying applied biology, there has been a debate among biologists about where the borderline of life is. There are two opinions. One is that viruses are the most basic life form and the other that bacteria are. Here's a simplified but accurate version of the argument ...

All biologists agree that to be considered "living" an organism must be able to eat, grow, and reproduce. If organisms can do these three things, they are living and if they can't, they are not living. Simple. So why the big argument? Well, you can take any bacteria in a laboratory, pop them in a petri dish with some food, and they will consume the food, get bigger, and multiply. Each virus, however, must be in a specific type of cell because they are specialized for precise environments. Put simply, they won't grow on any old gunk; they're picky about their food. Viruses are so precise that they can infect one type of animal only. So, for example, a virus that infects your cat cannot infect you. But they are even more exact than that and can invade just one type of tissue in a specific host species, so a virus that infects your lungs cannot affect your stomach.

OK, THAT'S INTERESTING BUT WHAT ABOUT CRYSTALS?
Well, crystals do eat, grow, and reproduce, but have to be in a very specific growing environment to do so. For example, quartz will grow in igneous rocks that are rich in readily available silicon and oxygen. This forms silicon dioxide, which grows as quartz crystals; and the more silicon and oxygen the quartz crystal eats, the bigger it gets. It eats! It grows! And we all really know this because you can see both little quartz crystals and big quartz crystals on display in crystal stores.

Quartz crystals reproduce in two ways. Firstly, if you take a quartz crystal and smash it into thousands of tiny fragments, each fragment will act as a seed crystal, when and if they are in the perfect silicon- and oxygen-rich growing environment. Remember, crystals are living in geological time, and sometime in the next five billion years that they have left on the planet (even if we humans won't last that long) it is guaranteed, due to natural geological processes, that every part of the earth's surface will at some point present the perfect growing environment for quartz crystals and your smashed-up crystal will reproduce into thousands of crystals.

Secondly, sometimes in nature a quartz crystal becomes dissociated from the rest of its crystal friends. This can happen physically due to rapid temperature changes or tectonic movement. Many years after this, often millennia or even millions of years later, the crystal starts eating again and begins to grow baby crystals at the point of fracture. These are called

Below: Crystals, such as this azurite, are living beings.

self-healed crystals and if you look closely it is easy to see the new baby crystals' terminations.

Not only do crystals have the ability to heal themselves, they are adept at healing us also. Most people agree that crystals can help many emotional and stress-related conditions, and thereby help to alleviate physical symptoms associated with them. Crystal healers believe that crystal healing goes much further and can help the body repair itself quicker than it otherwise would, and as such can theoretically help with almost any condition. If your body is capable of doing it, the correct crystals will help your body heal faster. They won't help what your body cannot do. For example, a crystal may help a bruise on your arm heal quicker and hurt less, but no crystal will help to regrow a lost limb. That's not to say that crystals will not be beneficial in dealing with the psychological and emotional distress associated with amputation.

In reality, we understand so little of how the body works. For example, no one

Above: As well as being beautiful, crystals hasten the speed the body can heal. Citrine helps to heal the digestive system.

knows how pain works. In fact, other than guesses, no one has a clue what happens in the synapse, the gap between nerves. So, according to Margo McCaffery,[3] medically, pain is defined as being whatever the person experiencing it says it is, existing whenever and wherever he/she says it does. Anyone who has experienced severe pain will tell you that there is nothing scientific about pain at all, or its treatment.

Another example is where you get your physical energy from. There is one biochemical reaction in the human body that produces significant quantities of energy. Adenosine triphosphate is converted to adenosine diphosphate and energy is released. The reaction is cyclical because as the energy is released the adenosine diphosphate converts back to adenosine triphosphate with the aid of an enzyme loop. This is simply expressed as ATP = ADP + Energy. It's brilliant and it is the only significant scientifically proved source of energy for the human body. So, according to science, it must produce all the energy you

Above: Simply having crystals around your home and workplace will bring benefits to your well-being. From left to right: lapis lazuli, spirit quartz, and smoky quartz are working together.

need. One problem, however, is that it produces about 20 percent of the energy that the body needs. Scientifically, there is no other major energy source for the human body. So what's the answer?

Perhaps it's the unmeasurable chi, ki, or Tao, or universal life-force energy, or more scientifically it might be called dark energy or dark matter. It is estimated that 75 percent of the universe is made up of dark matter that seems invisible to us. Among the latest areas of scientific research are the fields of dark energy and quantum physics, which suggest that the universe might actually be as wonderful (or weird) as some of us believe. Maybe further research into dark matter will eventually explain spirits appearing or walking through walls, clairvoyance, and healing. Maybe, as with light, crystals have the ability to affect dark matter. But however crystals work, it is clear that whenever someone undergoes a complete course of crystal healing, profound changes can happen, leading to improved well-being and the relief of symptoms. In fact, many of these things start to happen just by having crystals around you. The crystals you like, the ones you are drawn to, feeling their pull, these are the crystals you probably need right now. If you would like to find out more about crystal healing, visit www.thecrystalhealer.co.uk.

CRYSTAL GRIDS

A CRYSTAL GRID IS THE ARRANGEMENT OF ANY NUMBER OF CRYSTALS IN A GEOMETRIC PATTERN DESIGNED WITH A SPECIFIC FOCUS AND INTENT. CRYSTAL GRIDS CAN BE CREATED FOR ANY PURPOSE, NOTHING IS TOO TRIVIAL IF IT IS IMPORTANT TO YOU AND NOTHING IS TOO BIG THAT YOU CAN'T AFFECT IT. REMEMBER THAT IF A BUTTERFLY FLAPS ITS WINGS IN THE AMAZON RAINFOREST, IT CREATES A TINY DISTURBANCE IN THE AIR THAT CAN GENERATE A STORM THOUSANDS OF MILES AWAY IN THE USA OR EUROPE! AND IF ENOUGH PEOPLE WANT TO MAKE SOMETHING BETTER AND SEND THEIR FOCUSED THOUGHTS TOWARD THAT GOAL, THEN IT WILL HAPPEN QUICKER.

The crystals in the grid start to work as a team, each one playing the role and position they are suited to. As a team they generate more crystalline energy than they do individually, making the crystal grid more powerful than the sum of the individual crystals working alone.

Crystal grids are wonderful tools to help you work out what you really want and sort out the things you can do, which you have control over, and the things that are in the hands of the universe, which you feel you can't affect. Intent is one of the important keys to making any crystal grid and there are specific instructions in Chapter 3 on intention setting.

You are creating a very powerful psychological instrument that can give you a little boost when you need it or help you through the most challenging of times. Working with a crystal grid gives you something you can do about things you thought you could have no influence over.

Below: The simplest kind of crystal grid has just five crystals. Here, the crystal in the center, the focus stone, is fluorite and it is surrounded by larvakite, anyolite, carnelian, and tanzanite (clockwise from top).

WHAT IS A CRYSTAL GRID?

The arrangement of crystals in a grid, created with focus and intent, enhances the flow of energy in your life. It is a way of amplifying your intention by positioning crystals in an empowering sacred geometric pattern and is usually created with a specific outcome in mind, such as healing an injury or loss, or finding love or financial success.

Each variety of crystal has a natural healing energy of its own. By selecting crystals specifically for a chosen purpose and deliberately placing them in an enhancing sacred geometric shape (see page 16), they produce a small shift in subtle energy, leading to a specific outcome, sometimes massive in scale.

Opposite: Create your crystal grid for dreams (see page 78) next to your bed.

Anyone can make a crystal grid. The design can be quite ornate and complex, but the simplest has just five crystals, four arranged in a square with the fifth in the center (see image on previous page), for the purpose of directing energy toward a specific target, goal, result, or outcome. The stones or crystals are then charged by your intention and energy (see page 39), creating a very powerful psychological tool.

HOW AND WHY CRYSTAL GRIDS WORK

Crystals talk to each other! Yes, just like sound waves, they vibrate. In fact, they're in a continuous state of vibration. They also naturally tend toward balance and crystals can store, transmit, focus, amplify, and transmute energy. All this is scientifically proven and the information is openly and readily available online.

Crystals listen to each other and react to what they hear! Since crystals naturally bring energy to a harmonious point of balance, they settle the vibrations of all the crystals around them and when they are all focused with intent in one direction, with one deliberately assigned goal, they create a grid of energy that affects its surroundings. Like a pebble dropped into the ocean, the subtle effects are seen across the world.

The process of creating a crystal grid is psychologically empowering. In situations when it seems that there is nothing you can do, there ALWAYS is! In making a crystal grid with focused intent, you are compelling the universe to listen. This can work very simply and powerfully.

ENERGY FIELD OF A GRID

When you work with a single, naturally terminated crystal, such as a quartz crystal, it tends to channel energy in one direction through its termination since this is the direction of growth. Most rocks, such as rose quartz, which rarely forms large perfect crystals, are what can be called cryptocrystalline. This means they are made up of millions of microscopic-sized crystals growing in different directions. So the focus of the crystal's energy is more diffuse.

In a crystal grid, all the component crystals are arranged so as to focus their energy into the central "focus stone." Often the grid will be set up on a special geometric pattern, such as the flower of life or Metatron's cube (see pages 154 and page 155), which are said to be sacred, or perhaps something as simple as a circle or cube with a focus stone in the middle. The shape or pattern itself has an innate energy that will also amplify your intention. You can use any shape or symbol that has meaning to you, such as the chakra grid (see page 44), for self-healing or treating others but certain patterns are also sacred.

CONSTANT CONNECTION

Choose a special crystal to remind you of someone or something and carry it with you 24/7.

SACRED GEOMETRY

SACRED GEOMETRY HAS ITS ROOTS IN NATURE AND CAN BE SEEN IN THINGS SUCH AS THE
INTERNAL PATTERN OF A NAUTILUS SHELL GROWING AS A LOGARITHMIC SPIRAL PATTERN,
OR THE MATHEMATICAL RATIO OF SIZES AND SCALES IN THE HUMAN BODY AS OBSERVED
BY LEONARDO DA VINCI AND DESCRIBED IN HIS FAMOUS VITRUVIAN MAN DRAWING.

It is believed that these patterns run through the natural world, created from
ratios that are essential to the existence of life, and because of this they are
deemed to be designed by God, the Great Spirit, the Universal Life Force, the
Tao, or whatever name you choose to use. Hence the term "sacred geometry."
I am in no way being frivolous here but honoring your belief because sacred
geometry runs through ALL belief systems.

People who work with energy have noted that when these ratios are
expressed in art, they produce a noticeable and consistent energy pattern.
When you create your crystal grid on such a pattern, you are using the natural
energy of the mathematical ratios of life to enhance the energies of the crystals
and magnify the crystal grid's power. You can experiment with this yourself by
drawing simple patterns, such as a freehand circle and a perfect circle (you can

*Right: Perfect mathematical
ratios, such as a perfect
circle, can magnify the
power of a crystal grid.
This grid ensures safe
travel (see page 69).*

draw this with a compass or around a bowl or plate). Hold your hands an inch or two (2–5 cm) above your drawings, one above each, and try to sense the energy. Be patient and you will start to feel a tingling in the palms. If you don't feel it, try shaking your hands extremely vigorously for two minutes. This will bring the blood to the surface and optimize the sensation you feel. Then try holding your hands over each circle again. Notice the difference in the feeling between the perfect circle and the freehand one. Once you start to recognize these energies, try the same thing over the printed geometric patterns on pages 143–155.

If you're having difficulty recognizing these feelings in your hands, try measuring the energy patterns with a pendulum (see page 28 for more on pendulum dowsing). Hold the pendulum over the focus point of the grid and ask, "Show me the energy pattern." The pendulum will either start to circle or move in a straight line in a single plane depending on the grid you are looking at. As you become more proficient at pendulum dowsing you can discover the more intricate energy patterns of the flower of life and Metatron's cube (pages 154 and 155).

Below: Metatron's cube is one of the most powerful sacred shapes focusing energy into the center, the focus stone. If you are finding it difficult to solve a problem, this grid can help (see page 55).

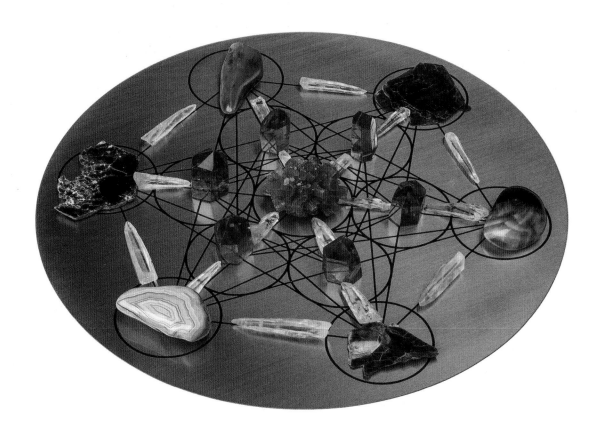

THE BENEFITS OF CRYSTAL GRIDS

ONE OF THE MOST AMAZING THINGS ABOUT CRYSTAL GRIDS IS HOW SIMPLE THEY ARE. PUT SOME CRYSTALS DOWN IN A GEOMETRIC PATTERN WHILE WISHING FOR YOUR DREAMS TO COME TRUE. IT'S AS SIMPLE AS THAT! AND CRYSTAL GRIDS CAN HELP YOU WITH ANYTHING AT ALL. IF YOU CAN IMAGINE IT, THEN THE RIGHT CRYSTAL GRID CAN HELP TO MAKE IT HAPPEN. IT MAY BE SOMETHING PERSONAL AND VERY PRIVATE, SOMETHING TO HELP EVERYONE IN YOUR HOME, OR SOMETHING SHARED WITH FRIENDS. IT MAY BE A BOOST FOR YOUR CAREER OR BUSINESS. WHATEVER IT IS, SOLVING YOUR PROBLEM, ENHANCING YOUR LIFE, AND FULFILLING YOUR DREAM IS JUST A FEW STEPPING STONES AWAY.

CRYSTAL GRIDS CAN BRING:

◊ Positivity, a positive feeling to everything you do

◊ Personal healing, regaining and maintaining health

◊ Cleansing negativity from your environment

◊ Focusing your goals

◊ Fulfilling your dreams

◊ Bringing your ideas into physical form

◊ Multiplying your personal power

◊ Discovering and growing caring, loving, passionate, sexually fulfilling relationships

◊ Help for you, your partner, family, and friends in your home

◊ Release of emotional blocks from the past

◊ Empowering you when you feel there is nothing you can do in a situation

◊ Help in taking your next step in life and moving forward

◊ Confidence, improved self-image

◊ Improved cognition, focus, memory, peace of mind

◊ Clearing the fog in your mind, allowing you to see your ideas clearly

◊ Better meditation, deeper meditation, more insightful meditation

◊ Reducing anxiety, depression, fear, moodiness, stress

◊ Destroying self-doubt

◊ Help in regaining control

◊ Better time management

◊ Boosting spiritual awareness

◊ Improved psychic abilities

◊ Creating prosperity

◊ Ripening new skills

◊ Regaining youthful energy and vitality

◊ Performing at your peak level

◊ Enjoying life more and living your dreams

◊ Freedom for yourself and others

BENEFITS CRYSTAL GRIDS CAN GIVE TO YOUR BUSINESS INCLUDE:

◊ More sales, customers, clients, patients, and the ones you actually want

◊ More profit

◊ More openings

◊ More creativity

◊ Finding the right employees

◊ Team building

◊ Creating a calm environment

◊ Security and safety

◊ Removing negativity from your business premises

◊ Expanding your business

TOURMALINE MEDICINE WHEEL

This is an example of how a crystal grid can work. The tourmaline medicine wheel crystal grid gives protection in any situation or place where its energies are focused, and to anyone.

My client, Tracey, was happily single and had an excellent financial job in the City of London. One day after work she came back to her out-of-town home to find she'd been burgled. The patio door had been carefully removed and every electronic device was missing, but nothing else had been touched. The burglars hadn't been through her closets and drawers, hadn't touched a single personal item, and had left no damage, except the patio door's hinges, not even a muddy footprint. She really didn't care. Everything was insured. Yes, Tracey did say losing the computer and having to change all her passwords was a pain in the backside (not quite her words), but she wasn't really bothered about it. She replaced everything and had the patio door fixed.

CRYSTALS FOR PROTECTION

Heliodor

Lapis lazuli

Pyrite

To find out more about these crystals and other crystals for protection, consult chapter 5, the crystal index (see page 122).

A few weeks later she came home from work to find she'd been burgled. The patio door had been carefully removed. Everything just replaced by the insurance had been stolen and nothing else had been touched! They hadn't been through her closets and drawers, hadn't touched a single personal item, and had left no damage, except the patio door's hinges, not even a muddy footprint.

This really spooked her out! So much so that she couldn't stay in her house overnight. I suggested she create a tourmaline medicine wheel crystal grid by her, now repaired, patio door. She went through the process with nine tourmaline crystals she'd carefully selected and by the time she'd finished (about 10 minutes) she felt okay to stay in her home again. This is the power of crystal grids. The crystals work and change the energy of a situation, and the process of creating the grid is psychologically empowering. Together this produces magic!

She has not been burgled again.

HOW TO CREATE YOUR TOURMALINE MEDICINE WHEEL

1 SELECT ONE VERY SPECIAL TOURMALINE CRYSTAL TO REPRESENT YOU OR WHAT IT IS YOU WANT TO PROTECT, such as your home when you're at work, or your car or your family. This is the focus stone. Select eight others to be part of the crystal grid so you have a total of nine tourmaline crystals. Nine is the number of universal love, the laws of karma and destiny.

2 NOW YOU WILL NEED TO IDENTIFY YOUR DIRECTIONS. You can either take a compass to mark the cardinal directions or you can simply say to yourself that you are creating a map, a representation, and in this case north is always at the top of the map. As you place the focus stone on the floor or a flat surface, think about its meaning, what or whom it represents, the purpose of the grid as a whole, and your intent. Take as much time as you need. Then create the medicine wheel around the focus stone as follows:

3 FIRST, SET A STONE TO THE NORTH, which represents the gods, or things that are out of your control. As you set this tourmaline crystal, ask whatever power or spirit you believe is represented by the north to protect you (or the focus of the crystal grid).

6 BEFORE YOU PLACE THE CRYSTAL IN THE EAST, fill in the gaps in the wheel with four of the remaining tourmaline crystals—northeast, northwest, southwest, southeast—so that when you place the ninth tourmaline crystal in the east, which is the gateway to the mind, the psychological, psychic, and spiritual worlds, you are closing the circle, completing the crystal grid, and empowering the situation, place, or people you want to protect.

4 NEXT, PLACE A STONE TO THE WEST, representing the physical world, which is often to do with money, careers, and finance, and ask whatever is there for you to protect you. If you believe you have one guardian angel or guide, ask him or her for support for every direction, but if you believe that different spirits or angels or deities look after different aspects of your life, call on those essences. Call on the spirit of the direction to help protect the focus of the crystal grid as you add each crystal to it.

5 THEN PLACE A STONE IN THE SOUTH, connecting to everything that is nurturing. For many people that's to do with home, family, and loved ones. Again, ask for help from your guardian spirit who resides in the south.

CHAPTER 2

CREATING A CRYSTAL GRID

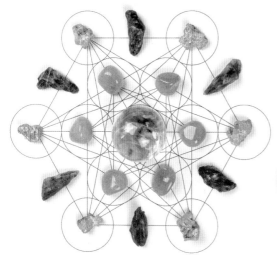

GETTING STARTED

SO NOW YOU UNDERSTAND A LITTLE MORE ABOUT CRYSTAL GRIDS, THE QUESTION IS—
HOW DO YOU SET UP YOUR OWN? YOU CAN, OF COURSE, GO STRAIGHT TO THE
CRYSTAL GRID PRESCRIPTIONS (SEE PAGE 46), BUT I RECOMMEND READING THIS SECTION
FIRST TO UNDERSTAND ALL THAT IS INVOLVED IN SETTING UP YOUR OWN CRYSTAL GRID.

Firstly, choose the purpose of your crystal grid. It might be to help you find
love or romance, or for healing yourself or another, or it may be for success in
a business venture or project, or anything else you like. Take a few moments
and jot down some thoughts around this idea.

What do you really want from it? What are the difficulties you are having or
might experience? Is there a sacred geometric shape or design that would help
to focus the energy of the grid? What color might support you? Some people
like to create an affirmation, a short positive phrase that they can chant or
repeat as they create and activate their grid to help to focus their intent. Some
people prefer to write this down on a small piece of paper that can be folded
and placed under the focus stone. Chapter 3 covers this in more detail.

*Right: You can create
a crystal grid for any
purpose you choose.
Here, angel aura quartz
is working with the
crystals surrounding it.*

SETTING UP YOUR GRID

CLEAR THE FOG

If you're feeling a little perplexed and finding it difficult to choose, hold a piece of chrysoprase to help clear the fog of a confused mind.

1 SELECT THE CRYSTALS YOU HAVE THAT MIGHT HELP THE PURPOSE YOU'VE CHOSEN (see Chapter 5); or you can work with the relevant crystal grid design in Chapter 4. If you're working with your own selection of crystals, choose one of them to represent the outcome you want. This will be the central crystal, the focus stone. If you have difficulty selecting the crystals you need, you can always ask your pendulum (see page 28).

2 THINK ABOUT THE PLACEMENT OF YOUR CRYSTAL GRID. Ideally, it should be situated somewhere it won't be disturbed but is easily accessible for you to activate and recharge from time to time (see page 30). If this is not practical, create the crystal grid on a tray, so you can put it in a safe place and have access to it when necessary. Alternatively, use a deep box picture frame that you can mount on the wall, and secure the crystals in place with white tack (or similar product) or a suitable adhesive if you want to keep these crystals working as a grid in perpetuity. You can come up with your own way of keeping the grid intact and moving it to a secure place where it won't be disturbed.

3 CLEANSE ALL THE CRYSTALS (see page 33) and mindfully place each one individually, focusing your thoughts and your intent on the outcome you want. As you create your grid you can repeat your affirmation either out loud or in your mind.

4 START BY PLACING THE FOCUS STONE IN THE CENTER OF THE GRID. Whether you're using a geometric grid or creating it freeform, without a template, place the focus stone in the center.

Right: Aqua aura is the focus stone in this example and represents the purpose of the grid.

5 THEN ADD THE FIRST RING OF CRYSTALS; this need not be in a circle, depending on your design. These are the crystals nearest to the focus stone, which will amplify and enhance the focus stone's exact energy meaning. Remember to focus on each crystal one at a time and repeat your affirmation out loud or in your mind as you place it in the grid.

Left: The first ring of crystals is made up of rose quartz. The first ring directs more relevant energy to the focus stone.

Right: Turquoise in the second ring fine-tunes the crystal grid.

6 ADD THE SECOND RING OF CRYSTALS IN THE SAME WAY; these can add detail to the energy of the crystal grid, making it even more focused. Keep your concentration on each crystal as you add it to the grid.

7 AMPLIFIERS ARE CRYSTALS PLACED BETWEEN THE ACTIVE CRYSTALS OF THE GRID to link two or more and to help the energy generated by the grid to flow easily toward the focus stone in the center. They are like stepping stones for your intention, directing the crystal energy of the grid and your thoughts toward their goal. They are often small, clear quartz crystals, but can be various specific crystals for any individual crystal grid; they are usually the same variety of crystal within any single grid (see Chapter 5).

Left: Amplifiers are crystal stepping stones, creating a path for your intent to follow. Here, the amplifiers are lapis lazuli.

8 YOU CAN ADD A PHOTOGRAPH OF A PERSON if the grid is for healing, or of your new dream house if you are looking to move, or you can write anything you like on a piece of paper and place it in or under or next to the crystal grid to help focus your thoughts.

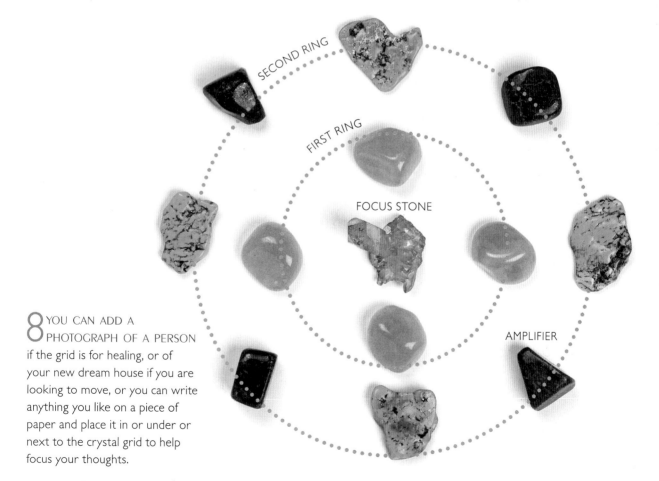

SECOND RING

FIRST RING

FOCUS STONE

AMPLIFIER

CRYSTAL COLOR AND SHAPE

THE COLORS AND SHAPES OF CRYSTALS CAN AFFECT THE FLOW OF ENERGY THROUGH
THE GRID. IF YOU HAVE POINTED CRYSTALS, ALWAYS TRY TO HAVE THE TERMINATIONS
POINTING DIRECTLY AT THE FOCUS STONE OR ANOTHER CRYSTAL *EN ROUTE* TO IT.
THINK OF IT AS CREATING CRYSTAL HIGHWAYS FOR THE ENERGY TO TRAVEL ALONG.

Crystals carved into other shapes, such as pyramids, cubes, merkaba, other geometric shapes, and animals, can all be centered as the focus stone.

The following charts give you the main shapes and colors, although the possibilities with both shades of color and variety of shape are almost endless.

FOCUS ON THE FOCUS STONE

Try to have a special crystal in the center of the grid for a focus stone. It's where all the energy is going so give it an easy target. Crystal spheres, clusters, and polished standing points are favorites. If it isn't possible to have something like this, still choose your stone carefully from the selection you have available. Your focus on this crystal will empower it and it will become special for you and your crystal grid.

CRYSTAL COLORS AND THEIR MEANING

COLOR		MEANING
RED		Passion, danger, positivity, survival, vitality
ORANGE		Energy, creativity, fertility
YELLOW		Happiness, prosperity, wisdom
GREEN		Art, emotions, growth, new beginnings
BLUE		Communication, truth, youth
INDIGO		Intuition, spirit, meditation
VIOLET	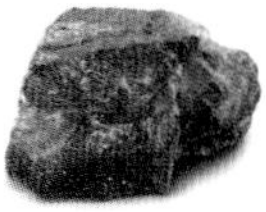	Spirituality, mystery, royalty

CRYSTAL SHAPES AND THEIR MEANING

Try observing the different energy patterns created by the various shaped crystals with your pendulum as described on page 28.

SHAPE		MEANING
ANIMALS		Connection to pet, totem, or spirit animal; movement
CUBE		Solid, supporting, reliability, building block
EGG		Birth, creation, new beginning or start of a project
HEART		Love, relationships, emotion
MERKABA		Visions, connection to higher realms
OBELISK		Connection between the physical and spiritual worlds
POINT		Focus and direction; positivity
PYRAMID		Energy fields, healing, meditation
SPHERE		Wholeness, completion, the world

PENDULUM DOWSING—A FRIENDLY AID TO CRYSTAL SELECTION

AT ANY POINT IN THE FOLLOWING PROCESS YOU MIGHT DOUBT YOUR
OWN INTUITION—EVERYONE DOES FROM TIME TO TIME, EVEN THE MOST
EXPERIENCED OF US—SO HERE'S A FAILSAFE CRYSTAL TIP TO HELP YOU:
MAKE FRIENDS WITH YOUR CRYSTAL PENDULUM!

Pendulum dowsing is simple and pendulums (sometimes called dowsers) made from crystal are the easiest to work with because the crystal amplifies the energy. Although quartz crystal is often preferred, you can choose whichever variety of crystal you fancy or feel drawn to.

If you aren't sure, go to a store where you can try various crystal pendulums for yourself. Discover your "yes" and "no" responses (see below), and then just ask the crystal pendulum if it is a good one for you to work with. If it says "yes," that's great! If not, then put it back and try another one. Once you have settled on your pendulum, you could employ it immediately in the store to select the crystals you need, either by passing the pendulum slowly over a selection of crystals and looking for your "yes" response, or holding a crystal in one hand and asking your pendulum if this crystal specifically is needed. For example, you can ask, "Is this a good crystal to have in my crystal grid for [add whatever the focus/purpose of the grid is]?"

You can use this method for all the crystals you need or just one or two you are uncertain of. Pendulums have so many other applications in your life since they'll basically answer any question that could have a yes/no reply.

HOW DO PENDULUMS WORK?

Your pendulum gives you an external visible response to something you already know. You can look at it in two ways: either there's a little bit deep inside you that knows everything or there's a little bit deep inside you that connects to the Divine and can sense the answer you are given. The Divine is whatever or whomever you believe is there for you. Watch an expert dowser closely and you'll see their arm or hand move a little, but the dowser is not doing it. The dowser has no control.

Everyone has an "internal pendulum," something deep inside that says "yes" or "no" to everything. Some people might call this gut feeling or woman's intuition, but everyone has it. Normally, we notice it in extreme circumstances only—the sinking feeling of "Oh no—get me out of here!" when you realize you shouldn't be where you are, or sense danger; the euphoric feeling of rising, unrestrained joy at your happiest "Wow!" moments. But your internal pendulum is saying "yes" and "no" to everything, all day long. It is saying it right now as you're reading this book! When you work with your pendulum, you simply see in front of you what is happening inside you. This gives you more confidence in your internal pendulum and the more you listen to it the stronger it becomes. In fact, the more you work with your crystal pendulum, over time, the less you will need it as you trust your inner pendulum more and more. Having said that, there are always some questions we come back to our crystal pendulum for because it is part of human nature to question everything, including ourselves.

You can identify your "yes" and "no" responses by asking your crystal pendulum two straightforward questions, such as "Am I a woman?" and "Am I a man?", or alternatively "Is grass green?" and "Is grass red?", and each time note how the pendulum moves. It will make two different movements, one for each answer. These may be clockwise or counterclockwise circles, moving back and forth or side to side. Watch carefully as these movements might initially be quite small and don't worry about how big the motion is because it will get clearer the more you work with the same crystal pendulum. If you prefer, you could ask any other pair of questions that have an absolute yes or no answer, such as using your name and another name—"Is my name X?" and "Is my name Y?"

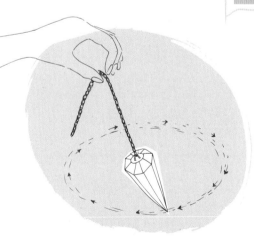

Above: Pendulum moving from side to side.

Above: Pendulum moving in a clockwise circle.

ACTIVATING YOUR CRYSTAL GRID

AS LONG AS YOU HAVE BEEN FOCUSED AND BUILT YOUR CRYSTAL GRID WITH INTENT IT WILL BEGIN TO WORK. HOWEVER, YOU CAN SUPERCHARGE YOUR GRID AND MAKE IT MORE POWERFUL BY ACTIVATING THE CRYSTALS INDIVIDUALLY AND THEN THE GRID AS A WHOLE. THE PURPOSE IS TO HELP YOU CONNECT WITH EACH OF THE CRYSTAL ELEMENTS OF YOUR GRID AND LINK THEM ENERGETICALLY TO THE FOCUS STONE, CREATING SIGNS AND PATHWAYS FOR THE ENERGY TO FLOW ALONG. THE CONNECTION OF EACH CRYSTAL TO THE FOCUS STONE HELPS THE CRYSTALS' COMMUNICATION AND ENHANCES THE WAY YOUR CRYSTAL TEAM PLAYS.

Right: A natural quartz crystal is preferred for your quartz master crystal.

To activate your grid you will need a quartz master crystal or crystal wand. A quartz master crystal can be either natural or polished. I prefer a natural, unpolished crystal for this task because it can sometimes be difficult to see whether a polished crystal is a natural shape that has been cleaned up and refined or if it is cut from broken crystal or rough rock. Remember, the energy flows naturally in the direction the crystal was originally growing (see page 14) and this is important in a master crystal because you will be working with it to focus and direct the energy of the crystal grid. If you are looking at a selection of cut and polished quartz crystal points in a store and they all look a similar shape, it is unlikely they have been cut from natural whole single crystals. What you are looking for is the natural variation in the facets of the termination and sides of the crystal. Very few natural crystals are even on all six sides and faces.

This is less important with a crystal wand since the intent of the person crafting it is to make it send energy in the one direction of the wand's focus.

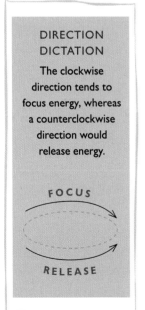

DIRECTION DICTATION

The clockwise direction tends to focus energy, whereas a counterclockwise direction would release energy.

FOCUS

RELEASE

1 CLEAR YOUR MIND OF ALL DISTRACTING THOUGHTS AND FOCUS SOLELY ON THE TASK IN HAND. Hold your quartz master crystal or wand about 2 inches (5 cm) above the focus stone in the center of your crystal grid and start to move it slowly in a small clockwise circle while chanting your positive affirmation.

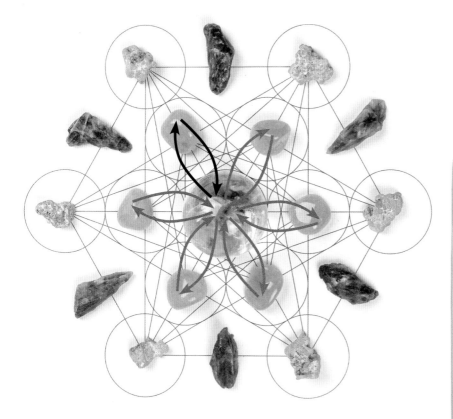

2 WHEN YOU BECOME AWARE OF AN ENERGY CHANGE IN THE
QUARTZ MASTER CRYSTAL OR WAND IN YOUR HAND, MOVE TO
THE NEXT CRYSTAL, that is the one on the inner circle toward the
top of the grid, and repeat the small clockwise circles and chanting.

The order in which the crystals should be activated is as follows:
Start at the central focus stone, move to the inner circle at the
top, then go back to the focus stone again—you have to reactivate
the focus stone after every other stone activation. Then move out
to the next crystal in the inner circle in a clockwise direction from
the last one you activated and back to the focus stone.

Each crystal should take less than two minutes to activate
initially, so if you find you're not registering a change in sensation,
move to the next crystal after a couple of minutes. The more you
practice the easier it is to feel these subtle energy changes.

CHANGING ENERGY

Different people
describe the feeling of
the energy change in
significantly contrary
ways. You may feel it
as the crystal heating
up or cooling down,
getting tingly or
stopping tingling, or
notice the shape in
which you're moving
the master crystal or
wand changing from
round to oval, or going
from feeling like it is
moving through treacle
to freeing up (or vice
versa). Whatever it is
you feel, all you need
to do is notice that
it feels different
from how it did when
you started.

3 AFTER ALL THE CRYSTALS IN THE INNER CIRCLE ARE ACTIVATED, CONTINUE IN THE SAME MANNER WITH THE SECOND RING and any other crystals in the grid, each time returning to reactivate and strengthen the connection of each crystal to the focus stone.

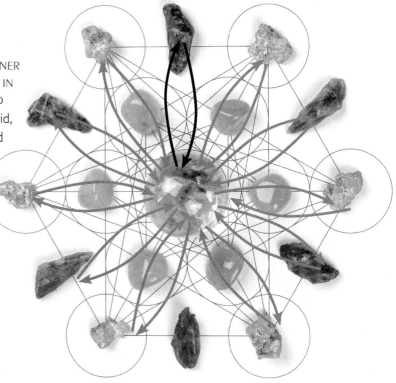

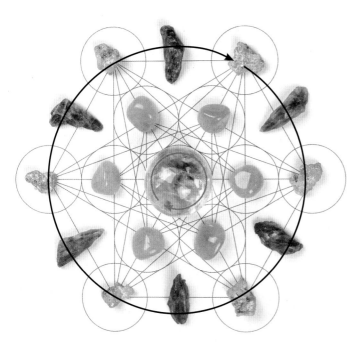

4 WHEN YOU HAVE ACTIVATED EVERY CRYSTAL INDIVIDUALLY, REPEAT THE PROCESS ONE MORE TIME for the crystal grid as a whole. Start at the focus stone, moving your quartz master crystal or wand slowly clockwise until you feel the energy change. Then move straight to the outermost crystal ring and circle the whole grid in a right-handed direction while chanting your positive affirmation.

CLEANSING YOUR CRYSTAL GRID

CRYSTAL GRIDS TEND TO HAVE A LONGER-TERM PURPOSE THAN WHEN WE WORK WITH INDIVIDUAL CRYSTALS, SO WE NEED TO TREAT THEM A LITTLE DIFFERENTLY WHEN IT COMES TO CLEANSING AND AVOID METHODS THAT WOULD INVOLVE TAKING THE GRID APART BEFORE ITS WORK IS COMPLETED, SUCH AS HOLDING THE CRYSTALS UNDER RUNNING WATER.

Once your grid is set up and activated, the crystals in it are working as a team and it is best not to disturb them. By far the easiest and most effective way to cleanse your crystal grid is with sound. I prefer using tingsha (Tibetan cymbals) but you can just as easily use a drum, bell, singing bowl, or any other spiritual musical instrument. With tingsha, play them over the center of the grid and allow the sound to vibrate any stagnant energy from the crystals and out of the grid.

Once the crystal grid has fulfilled its purpose, you can dismantle it and cleanse the crystals individually using any of the methods described below.

CLEANSING CRYSTALS

Crystals need to be cleansed for several reasons. When you work with crystals, either by yourself or with others, they absorb energy from you, other people, and their environments. They can also become dusty and lackluster. You can see when your crystals need cleansing—they lose their sparkle, brightness, and even color. Crystals in need of cleansing may also feel sticky to the touch.

GOOD ENERGY VERSUS BAD ENERGY

Crystals naturally pick up energy from the environments they live in. Any traditional crystal cleansing method, from sunlight to running water (see pages 34–35), removes surplus energy that they have absorbed, and which is no longer needed.

Right: There is no such thing as good or bad crystals—jet (top) and petalite both channel healing energy.

We may often seek to define this absorbed energy as good or bad, but there really is no difference between the two—energy is simply energy, without judgment. Native American peoples used obsidian to fashion arrowheads just as healers recommend holding the stone to the belly to ease stomach ache. The ancient Greeks used beautiful quartz crystal globes to

cauterize wounds, but leave one in direct sunlight and the same energy may burn your house down. So do not be concerned that your crystals somehow possess innate good or bad energy; they have only energy, and cleansing them helps release energy build-up, preparing them for healing work.

REMOVING DUST

Crystals do become dusty. Dust sticks with an electrostatic charge that affects the special electricity-generating properties of crystals. Dusty crystals will not work as effectively as crystals that have been cleansed, and dust also blocks light, which reduces the quantity of photons a crystal can focus. To remove dust, lightly brush your crystals with a soft brush—a make-up brush or small paintbrush is ideal. Do this regularly to avoid dust build-up.

CLEANSING METHODS

You can cleanse your crystals by placing them in a bowl and immersing them in a solution of water and a little mild detergent. Afterward, rinse them thoroughly with water to make them sparkle. Leave your crystals to dry naturally or pat them gently with a soft cloth.

Here are some of the other traditional ways of cleansing crystals. If your crystals are water-soluble, don't use a cleansing technique that involves water!

◊ RUNNING WATER—hold your crystal under running water for a few minutes. It may need longer if it's been working hard or hasn't been cleansed for a long time.

◊ MOONLIGHT—leave your crystal in moonlight, especially the light of a full or new moon.

◊ EARTH—bury your crystal in the earth and leave it there for one to two weeks or moon cycles. Bury it when the moon is full and unearth it at the time of a new moon.

◊ CRYSTAL CLEANSING—place your crystal on an amethyst bed or quartz cluster, or inside a geode.

◊ SUNLIGHT—leave your crystal in sunlight. You can also dry your crystals in the sun after washing them. Beware, though—quartz crystals, especially crystal balls, will focus the sun's rays and can be a fire risk. Take appropriate precautions by not leaving quartz unattended in sunlight for any length of time, and do not place on or near any flammable objects.

Above: You can cleanse your crystals under running water.

Above: Take care when cleansing any quartz crystal in sunlight, as it will focus the sun's rays and can be a fire risk.

Above: If cleansing crystals using smoke, frankincense, sandalwood, and sage smoke are best.

◊ SOUND—clear your crystal of unwanted vibrations by chanting or drumming or using tingsha (Tibetan cymbals).

◊ BREATH OR LIGHT—exposing your crystal to your breath or light is cleansing. You can also practice reiki on your crystal.

◊ INCENSE—let frankincense, sandalwood, or sage smoke waft over your crystal. You can use a smudge stick to do this (a smudge stick is a small bundle of herbs that is burnt during cleansing rituals).

Above: Only cleanse the crystals in a grid individually once its work is completed. This crystal grid is for awareness (see page 82).

AN ENERGIZING CRYSTAL GRID

You can energize an event or idea, concept or goal with this crystal grid and carefully chosen focus stone. It takes you a step further and can speed up and enhance the process. It can be particularly helpful with non-tangible concepts and ideas, or events distanced from you by time and space, such as finding a parking space (important in UK, less so in Arizona), your sports team winning a match, baking a cake to perfection, finding an answer in your meditation.

You will need six quartz crystal points and a focus stone. Choose one specifically to help your intent for the crystal grid (see Chapter 5). We work with six crystals as they will represent the natural six sides of all quartz crystals. Six is the number of healing and quartz crystal is the archetypical healing crystal. Place them with their terminations pointing inward as if they were making up the six corners of a hexagon. You might like to draw a hexagon on a piece of paper and place the crystals in the six corners. Now put the focus stone in the center of this crystal grid. You can also add a photograph or written request if these feel relevant. Some people like to secure the crystals in position. If you want to do this, I suggest using white tack (or a similar product) or double-sided tape that will not damage the crystals. If you really feel you need to use an adhesive, be gentle with your crystal friends. Once you are happy with your arrangement, you can ask your crystals to help, in this example, say to find the parking space for you, and since this will be set up permanently, to continue to find you parking spaces!

No concept is too trivial or too important for a crystal grid. The possibilities are endless and although mysterious, the positive outcomes make life happier and easier.

CRYSTALS FOR
ENERGIZING
YOUR IDEA

Focus stone:
amethyst

Quartz
crystal

PLACE QUARTZ CRYSTALS WITH THEIR
TERMINATIONS POINTING INWARD

PUT THE FOCUS STONE IN
THE CENTER

CHAPTER 3

INTENTION SETTING

PREPARING

INTENT IS VERY IMPORTANT WHEN CONSTRUCTING A CRYSTAL GRID. IT IS ALSO IMPORTANT IN ALMOST EVERYTHING YOU DO EACH DAY, FROM GETTING UP IN THE MORNING TO GOING TO SLEEP AT NIGHT. IT TELLS THE UNIVERSE WHAT YOU WERE MEANING TO DO EVEN IF YOU'VE GOT IT A LITTLE WRONG TODAY. AND SETTING YOUR INTENTION IS SIMPLE TO DO—CLEAR AND FOCUS YOUR MIND AND SET YOUR DESIRE —BUT DESPITE, OR MAYBE BECAUSE OF, ITS SIMPLICITY, INTENT IS A VERY POWERFUL TOOL.

From time to time we all find ourselves in a position where we feel there is little or nothing we can do to influence a situation or people, such as when your kids go traveling alone or with friends and you are at home worrying, or your partner flies off on a business trip. We feel stuck and powerless or, worse, trapped. These feelings are created because our mind is telling us we cannot do anything, we are helpless, useless, without meaning or function, which is, understandably, depressing. That makes us feel bad, low, down. If this persists, it can lead to disharmony between body and mind, eventually expressed in disease or illness. Of course, in your mind there appears to be little or nothing you can do, other than worry, as if the act of worrying may in some way possibly solve the problem, even though you know deep down inside that it won't.

STOP! It's time to create a crystal grid. We're going to use all this amazing "worry energy" you have built up to create the intent to power your crystal grid and keep your bit of the universe on track.

Great side effects of focusing your intent into a crystal grid include calmness, relaxation, stress relief, improved skin and skin conditions. Digestive problems are relieved or disappear, minor aches and pains vanish, sometimes long-term chronic conditions get unexpectedly better, and your mind stops aimlessly wandering and you can think, focus, and function again.

Let's split the process down into sections to make it easier to explain. Firstly, choose a suitable time and find a place where you won't be disturbed. Put up a "Do not disturb" sign either physically or figuratively. Tell people around you, family, friends what you are doing and ask them not to disturb you, and make sure any children or pets have something to occupy them. Switch off your phone. These few steps make a useful exercise in themselves. Although it can take a real effort to create your own space, it's worth it in the end for the benefits it will bring. You can just enjoy being alone in your own undisturbed world, free from external influence for a little while if you like.

EXTERNAL DISTURBANCES

If you have external disturbances, such as noisy neighbors, place pyrite crystals against the windows, doors, or walls where the noise is coming from. Within a few minutes this will almost miraculously stop the noise disturbing you.

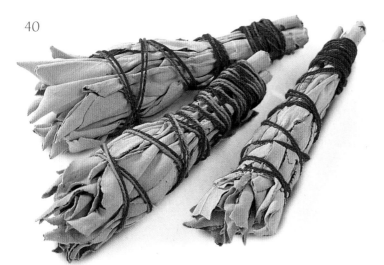

Above: A sage stick is wonderful for cleansing unwanted energies from your space.

If the room or space is normally used for other activities, such as a bedroom, office, play area, or dining area, you may feel you need to cleanse the energy before you start so as to make it completely your own space for the time being. You can do this in many different ways but one of the most reliable is burning a sage smudge stick and directing the smoke from the herb into each corner of the room, traditionally with a feather or feather fan, to clear the space of unwanted energies. Hold something under the smoldering sage stick to catch any embers that may fall. Traditionally this is a seashell (I have an abalone shell), which ties in very nicely with the spirit elements Earth represented by the sage stick, Air by the feathers, Fire by the smoke, and Water by the seashell. In Native American Indian tradition, feathers carry our prayers to Spirit and smudge ceremonial fans are usually made from either eagle or red-tailed hawk feathers because these are the birds that fly highest in the sky and therefore carry our prayers closer to the Spirits. (Please note, trade in eagle feathers is protected by the CITES Treaty and therefore most commercially available smudge fans and feathers use natural or painted feathers that simulate eagle and red-tailed hawk feathers.)

You can also make the space special by bringing in crystals, flowers, colorful things, and pictures of people or places that are important to you. You are now ready to begin ...

STILLNESS

Finding a place of quiet within you in today's fast-moving world can be a challenge in itself. Learning to find inner stillness is something that will benefit you not just in building crystal grids but also in many other aspects of your daily life. The first thing to do is breathe. Really breathe and know that you are breathing. Take a slow deep in-breath, and in your mind, watch the air as it passes the tip of your nose, comes up through your nostrils, reaches the back of your throat, slowly drops down your windpipe, and fills your lungs from the diaphragm in your belly up to the top of your chest. Take a few breaths like this. As you slow down, notice that the world around you becomes relaxed and unhurried.

AMETHYST AWARE

Hold an amethyst crystal in the palm of each hand while you focus on your breathing. Still focusing on your breath, just allow yourself to be aware of the amethyst crystals in the palms of your hands as you breathe.

CLARITY

Once you feel a stillness within you, the next challenge is to clear your mind completely of everyday concerns. For this you will need a meditation crystal. This can be any type of crystal, and any shape you choose. I like to work with a natural clear quartz Lemurian crystal for meditation. However, occasionally I will choose a different one for a specific task.

Hold your meditation crystal and look at it. Take your time and really look at it so you can memorize it and fix the image in your mind. Close your eyes and see the image of your crystal in the middle of your mind. If it is not clear, open your eyes and look at your crystal again, allowing your brain to fix the image in your mind. Repeat this stage until you can hold a clear image of your crystal in your mind. The more you practice this the easier it becomes and you will get to the point where you know the crystal so well that you won't even need it with you to place the image in your mind.

Imagine your crystal in the middle of your mind ... see it spinning very, very slowly. Allow yourself to be aware of your thoughts and focus your mind on any one thought. See this thought drift toward your crystal, which is spinning very, very slowly in the middle of your mind, and watch your thought disappear into the crystal. It's as if the crystal has magically absorbed the thought. Breathe. Focus on another thought and watch that one as it floats toward your slowly spinning crystal and disappears into it. Continue this process with one thought at a time until there are no more thoughts in your head and your mind is clear and ready to focus on the task at hand.

FOCUS

Once you feel still and clear you are in a place to start to set your desire. You need to be still and clear or else all manner of thoughts, feelings, memories, and mind-conversations within your normal everyday mind will influence and depreciate the power of your intention.

Grab a pad of paper and pen, concentrate on the single thought of the focus for your crystal grid, such as a new job or relationship, or healing yourself or others, and write this down. Then focus your mind on this single thought until another word or phrase comes into your mind and write that down. Return your mind's attention to the focus of your crystal grid. Keep going, allowing more words and phrases to come one by one, writing down each new word or phrase before returning your mind to your crystal grid focus each time until you are happy that you understand the intention clearly yourself. These are your empowerment notes. This process uses that amazing "worry energy" that was blocking you at the beginning and converts it into a supertool for your empowerment!

AMBER AID

Amber aids memory. So if it is not practical to keep your meditation crystal with you all the time, carry a small piece of amber with you to help you recall the image of your meditation crystal in your mind.

Even in the twenty-first century, with all the technology around you, it is important here to work with pen and paper because in the act of writing, the ink channels your energy into the paper and creates a physical presence. If you have to work on a computer, tablet, phone, or another device that may be available in the future, be sure to print the document to achieve a similar effect.

Once you have your intention clear in your own mind, try to reduce it to a simple phrase you can repeat as a mantra as you activate your crystal grid. For example, if your desire is to find a new home and you are looking for a four-bedroomed house for you and your family to live in, with a garden, in a suburban area, near a good school and local shopping, with access to good travel links, your mantra might be as simple as "Find a new home for me." You will have included all the other details in your thoughts and empowerment notes, so "Find a new home for me" includes four bedrooms, your partner and children, garden, type of area, access to school, shops, and travel links, and anything else you've thought through this process that you will need.

Take up your quartz master crystal and chant to it your newfound mantra. It is purely personal choice if you wish to chant out loud or inside your head. After a little while your quartz master crystal will let you know it has got your message. It will start to buzz or hum or vibrate or shine—whatever your crystal does and however this feels to you, you will recognize this as the sign that it is ready to start activating your crystal grid.

Below: Your quartz master crystal will let you know when it understands your intent.

Opposite: Like a sports team, every crystal has its role in a crystal grid. Here, the team will bring you insight into situations (see page 104).

HOW TO CREATE A CRYSTAL CHAKRA HEALING GRID

This crystal grid is designed for self-healing or treating others. It is also great as a general tonic to keep you well and ward off any bugs and colds that are around. To start, why not create it for yourself? You can work with the recommended crystals or select your own for each chakra. When you build this for a specific condition for yourself or another, it's a good idea to select crystals that might benefit the condition (see Chapter 5).

Photocopy the template on page 145 at 200% or print it out from www.thecrystalhealer.co.uk (see note on page 143). Make sure you have your crystals to hand. If you're working with the suggested ones, you will have amethyst, lapis lazuli, blue lace agate, malachite, citrine, carnelian, and red jasper, and 28 quartz crystals.

It is important to empty your mind and focus on your intent for the crystal chakra healing grid (see Chapter 3). With your mind concentrated on the task at hand, start by placing the chakra crystals on each chakra, beginning with the amethyst crystal on the crown, then the lapis lazuli on the brow until all seven chakras are covered. Now place four quartz crystals around each chakra crystal with their terminations pointing in toward the chakra crystal to form a cross pattern. These will help to amplify your intent even more and focus each chakra crystal's energy.

Place each crystal in its position with focus and care. Once you have placed all the crystals you have completed the crystal chakra healing grid. You can leave it undisturbed to carry on doing its work or you can activate the grid for even more power (see page 30).

The grid will continue to pump out healing energy as long as you want it to but it is recommended to reactivate it from time to time and especially whenever an extra healing boost is required.

Left: Place four quartz crystals around each chakra crystal.

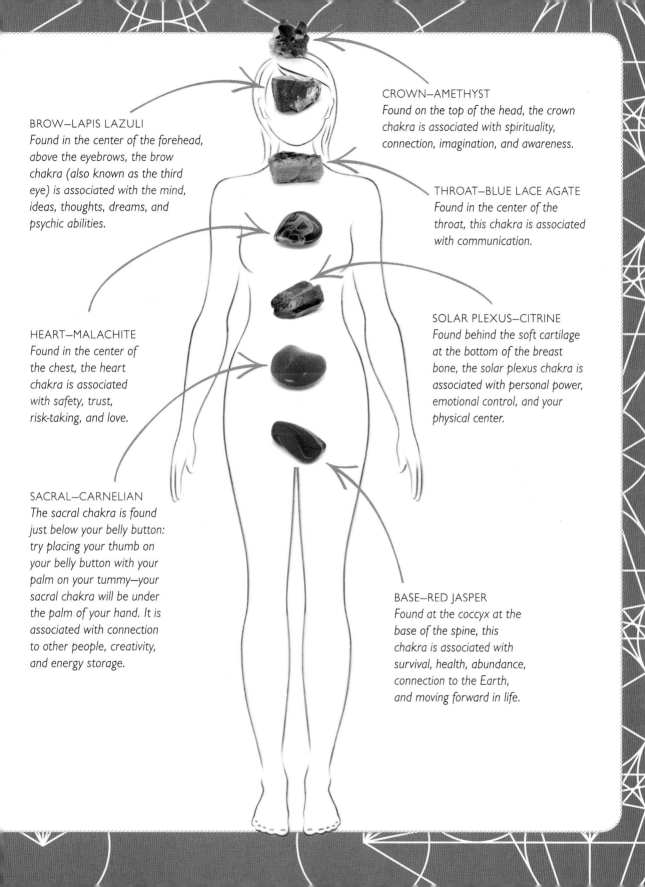

CROWN—AMETHYST
Found on the top of the head, the crown chakra is associated with spirituality, connection, imagination, and awareness.

BROW—LAPIS LAZULI
Found in the center of the forehead, above the eyebrows, the brow chakra (also known as the third eye) is associated with the mind, ideas, thoughts, dreams, and psychic abilities.

THROAT—BLUE LACE AGATE
Found in the center of the throat, this chakra is associated with communication.

HEART—MALACHITE
Found in the center of the chest, the heart chakra is associated with safety, trust, risk-taking, and love.

SOLAR PLEXUS—CITRINE
Found behind the soft cartilage at the bottom of the breast bone, the solar plexus chakra is associated with personal power, emotional control, and your physical center.

SACRAL—CARNELIAN
The sacral chakra is found just below your belly button: try placing your thumb on your belly button with your palm on your tummy—your sacral chakra will be under the palm of your hand. It is associated with connection to other people, creativity, and energy storage.

BASE—RED JASPER
Found at the coccyx at the base of the spine, this chakra is associated with survival, health, abundance, connection to the Earth, and moving forward in life.

CHAPTER 4

CRYSTAL GRID PRESCRIPTIONS

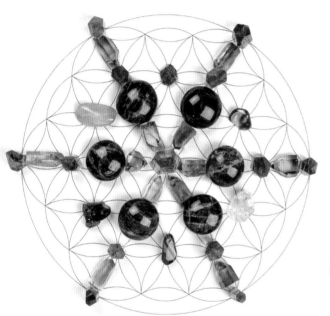

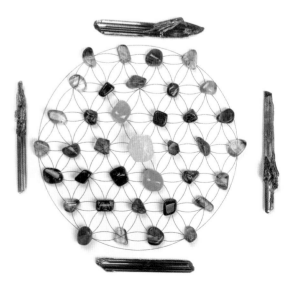

HOW TO WORK WITH
THE PRESCRIPTIONS

THESE CRYSTAL GRID PRESCRIPTIONS HAVE BEEN CREATED TO HELP YOU FACE LIFE'S CHALLENGES. IF YOU DON'T HAVE ALL THE PRESCRIBED CRYSTALS, SIMPLY BEGIN WITH THE ONES YOU ALREADY HAVE IN A SIMPLIFIED VERSION OF THE GRID LAYOUT AND ADD THE OTHERS OVER TIME AS YOU ACQUIRE THEM. YOU WILL START TO SEE THE BENEFITS QUICKER THAN WAITING UNTIL YOU HAVE ALL THE RELEVANT CRYSTALS.

In this chapter, you will discover fifty unique crystal grids divided for ease into sections for Lifestyle Enhancement, Spiritual Enhancement, Emotional Challenges, and Physical Healing, together with an easy-to-follow illustrated instruction guide to each crystal grid's creation.

It is important to keep your focus and intent during the whole setting up process, so, as described in Chapter 3 (see pages 38–43), choose a suitable time and place, put up your "Do Not Disturb" sign, whether real or imaginary, and TURN OFF YOUR PHONE! Tell anyone else who is around that you're not to be disturbed and make sure pets and children are calm and that everyone has all their needs met and won't interrupt you.

Start by selecting the crystal grid prescription you need and jot down some of your thoughts and feelings around the subject. What do you really want from your crystal grid? Are there any obstacles that might get in your way?

Use the geometric shape prescribed with the grid. You will find these in the Sacred Geometry section (pages 143–155) and can copy them on a photocopier, also enlarging them if you have the facility. These are also available as a free download from my website, www.thecrystalhealer.co.uk. The grids without prescribed geometry—i.e. freeform— are designed to be flexibly created whenever and wherever you need them. You can easily add any color you are drawn to by using colored paper when you print your crystal grid templates.

Write an affirmation to chant or place under the crystal grid to help focus your thoughts. For example, with the crystal grid for Love and Romance (see page 96), it might be as simple as "Love, love, love" or more specific like "Help find me the perfect partner..." (and you can then list all the attributes such a wonderful person would have). You can also add a photograph—for example, of a person or pet you have in your thoughts if the grid is for Health and Healing (see page 119).

When you are ready, clear all your other thoughts and focus your mind (see Chapter 3), take a deep breath, and as you breathe out start by placing the focus stone in the center of the grid.

Follow the guide on pages 24–25 to build the rest of the grid. Remember to focus on each crystal one at a time, take a deep breath, and repeat your affirmation out loud or in your mind as you place the crystal in the grid.

LIFESTYLE ENHANCEMENT

Above: Learning, page 60

Above: Children, page 58

Below: Justice, page 56

CAREER

Whether you are starting a new job, going back to work after a break, making a change in direction, or embarking on a completely new career, try this crystal grid to bring focus and clarity to your thoughts and power to your intention.

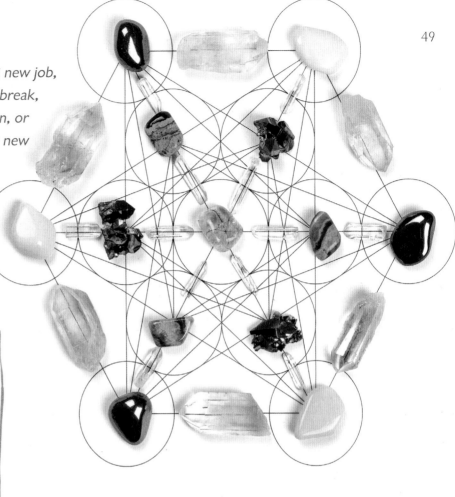

CRYSTAL TIP

You can use whatever size quartz you have available. In this grid, I have placed 6 large crystals and 12 small.

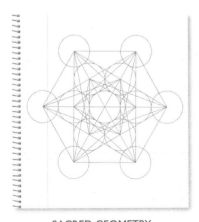

SACRED GEOMETRY
Metatron's cube (see page 155)

FOCUS STONE

Citrine

FIRST RING CRYSTALS

Titanium quartz × 3

Bumble bee jasper × 3

SECOND RING CRYSTALS

Hematite × 3

Snow quartz (white quartz) × 3

AMPLIFIERS

Quartz crystals × 18

ABUNDANCE

Whatever you need more of, you can bring it into your life. This crystal grid will really help you to focus your intentions, whether what you want is an abundance of wealth or of friends and fun.

Above: Citrine is the focus stone.

SACRED GEOMETRY
Flower of Life (see page 154)

FOCUS STONE

Citrine

FIRST RING CRYSTALS

Citrine x 6

SECOND RING CRYSTALS

Ruby x 6

Tiger's eye x 6

THIRD RING CRYSTALS

Citrine x 5—place one at each of the four cardinal points, and there is also one in the ring.

Magnetite

Dioptase

Spirit quartz

Sunstone

Tiger's eye

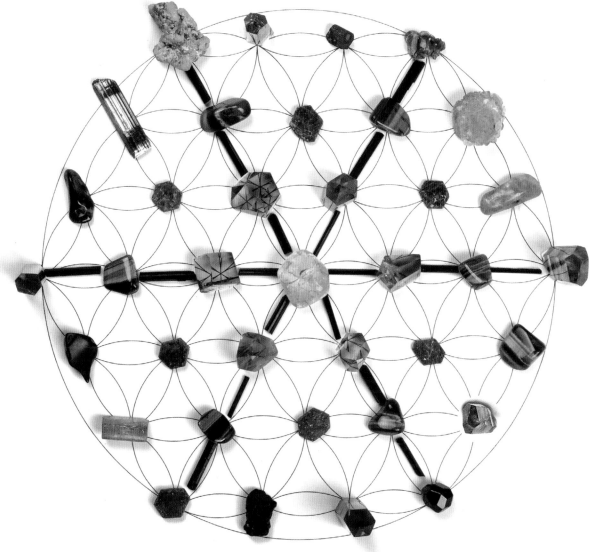

Garnet

Topaz

Stibnite

Tektite

Jet

Turquoise

Ruby

Green
moss agate

Green tourmaline × 18

CREATIVITY

Writing, art, design, music, dance, acting ... in fact any kind of performance or display will benefit from this healing spiral of creative energy.

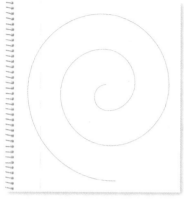

SACRED GEOMETRY
Spiral (see page 151)

FOCUS STONE

Citrine

FIRST RING CRYSTALS
Continue the spiral from the focus stone with the following crystals.

 Cryolite

 Fluorite

 Pyrite

 Turquoise

 Crocoite

 Alexandrite

 Quartz

 Chrysocolla

 Ruby

 Black moonstone

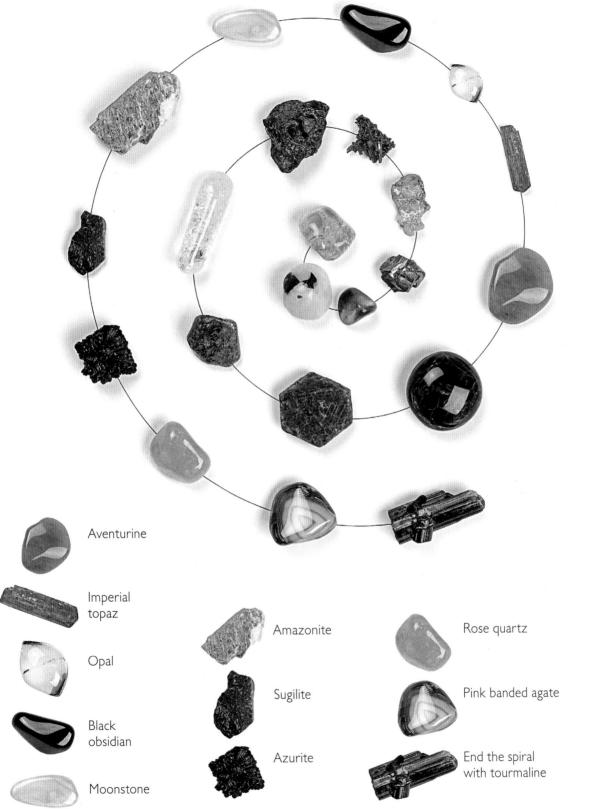

Aventurine

Imperial
topaz

Opal

Black
obsidian

Moonstone

Amazonite

Sugilite

Azurite

Rose quartz

Pink banded agate

End the spiral
with tourmaline

PUBLIC SPEAKING

Even great orators can get nervous before speaking in public, and if you're not experienced, it can be really scary! Standing up there with everyone looking at you expectantly can make you want to run away and hide ...

SACRED GEOMETRY Freeform

FOCUS STONE

Amethyst

FIRST RING CRYSTALS

Turquoise × 2

Septarian × 2

AMPLIFIERS

Kyanite × 4

PROBLEM-SOLVING

Find the answers you need! Many people say that when working with this crystal grid, answers just pop into their mind as if they were always there ... which, of course, they were.

SACRED GEOMETRY
Metatron's cube
(see page 155)

FOCUS STONE

Aragonite

FIRST RING CRYSTALS

Citrine × 6

SECOND RING CRYSTALS

Banded amethyst

Jade

Pink banded agate

Muscovite × 3—place between the other crystals of this ring

AMPLIFIERS

Quartz crystals × 18

The grid for problem-solving can also be seen on page 17.

JUSTICE

*This one helps you to focus your mind on a fair outcome.
Not only is it perfect for any major legal situation, it works
just as well for disputes among family, friends, and neighbors.
You can create this one for yourself to bring a favorable
outcome in litigation, but if it involves friends or family, try
sitting down with them and creating the grid together for
a fair and just outcome for all.*

SACRED GEOMETRY
Square (see page 150)

FOCUS STONE

Amethyst

FIRST RING CRYSTALS

Jade x 4—place one
in each corner of
the square

AMPLIFIERS

Amethyst x 20

*This grid can also be
seen on page 48.*

NETWORKING

In today's society, the power to connect with people may be seen as essential, whether it's face to face or through social media, one to one or in large groups. Simply focus your mind to create your crystal grid for networking, activate it, and see those connections come flooding in!

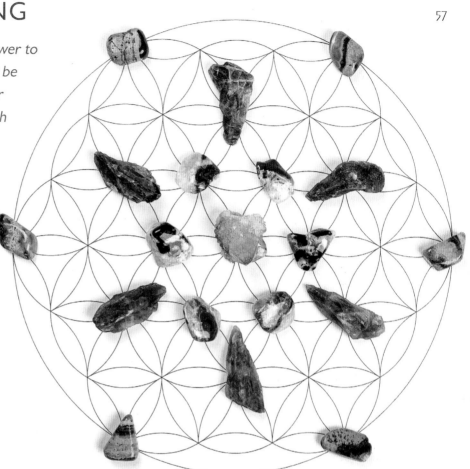

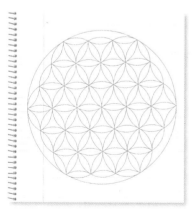

SACRED GEOMETRY
Flower of life (see page 154)

FOCUS STONE

Spirit quartz

FIRST RING CRYSTALS

Purple ray opal x 6

SECOND RING CRYSTALS

Super seven x 6

THIRD RING CRYSTALS

Bumble bee jasper x 6

CHILDREN

Kids can be the joy of your life, and they can also be a source of perpetual worry for at least their first fifty years! You want to protect them from harm and give them freedom to find themselves. You don't want to let them out of your sight but want them to explore by themselves. Life with children is full of contradictions. Give them the benefit of the knowledge and wisdom you've gained the hard way, but allow them to stand on your shoulders and grow rather than stifling them by covering them with your wings. Nurture and protect them on their journey and find the right words for both you and them.

FLOWER OF LIFE
(see page 154)

FOCUS STONE

Sugilite

FIRST RING CRYSTALS

Red jasper x 2

Chrysocolla x 2

Jade x 2

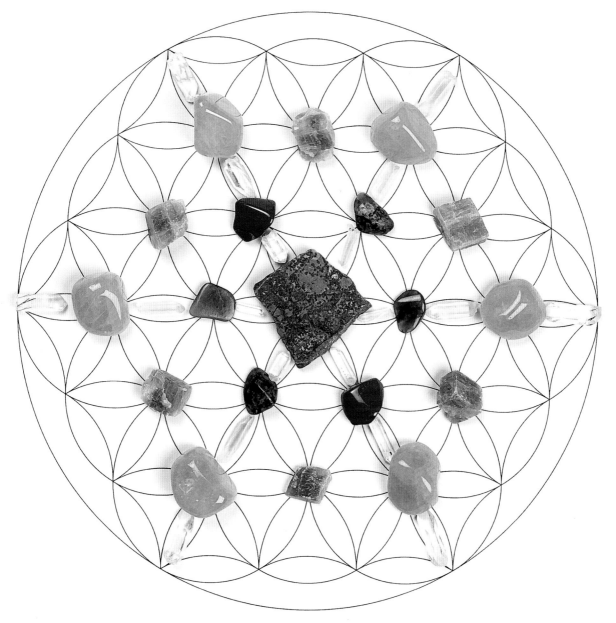

The grid for children can also be seen on page 48.

SECOND RING CRYSTALS

 Blue calcite × 6

 Rose quartz × 6

AMPLIFIERS

 Quartz crystals × 18

LEARNING

If you are studying for exams, or thirst for knowledge for its own sake, or undertake any other type of learning, creating this crystal grid will help. It enables you to clear your mind of distractions, focus your thoughts on the task at hand, and assimilate and remember what it is you learn.

SACRED GEOMETRY
Flower of life (see page 154)

Above: Moonstone is used in the second ring of this grid to bring flow to your learning process.

FOCUS STONE

Citrine

FIRST RING CRYSTALS

Sugilite

Jade

Ruby

Aquamarine

Lepidolite

Obsidian

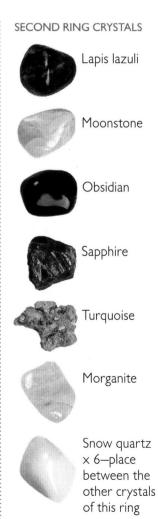

SECOND RING CRYSTALS

Lapis lazuli

Moonstone

Obsidian

Sapphire

Turquoise

Morganite

Snow quartz x 6—place between the other crystals of this ring

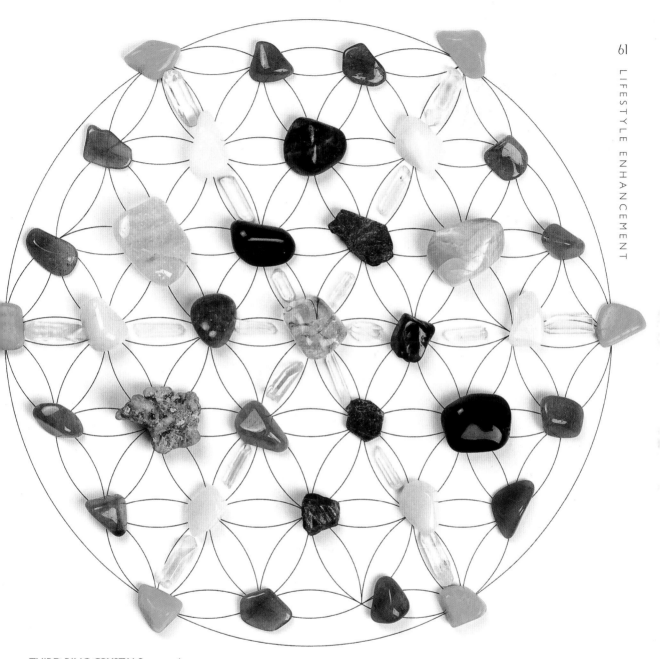

THIRD RING CRYSTALS

 Amazonite

 Aventurine

AMPLIFIERS

 Quartz crystals
× 18

*The grid for learning can
also be seen on page 48.*

LEADERSHIP

When you need to step forward and lead from the front, when you need a lion's strength while retaining the gentleness of an angel to spearhead the challenges your team are presented with, these are the times to draw upon the power of the leadership crystal grid.

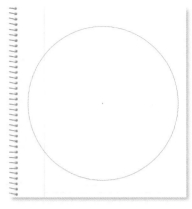

SACRED GEOMETRY
Circle (see page 143)

FOCUS STONE

Aventurine

_____

FIRST RING CRYSTALS

Pyrite x 8

_____

AMPLIFIERS

Aventurine x 20

TEACHING

Do you need the confidence to share your knowledge? Are you teaching in a different way, maybe at a new school, center, or venue? Set up this grid when you prepare, practice, and teach your class, starting from scratch each time and putting your essence into both the grid and the teaching space.

SACRED GEOMETRY Freeform

FOCUS STONE

Citrine

FIRST RING CRYSTALS

Blue calcite

Green calcite

Golden calcite

Red calcite

SECOND RING CRYSTALS
Place at the major cardinal points.

White calcite

Orange calcite

Black calcite

Honey calcite

Link these crystals by alternating:

Citrine

Blue calcite

I've placed five stones in between each of the major calcites but you can have more or less, depending on availability and space.

AMPLIFIERS

Stibnite x 4

NEW BEGINNINGS

A new job, a change of career, a new relationship, a completely fresh start in life—there's always a need for this grid. You can set it up and take it down, cleanse it and reset it for a new beginning whenever you like.

SACRED GEOMETRY
Flower of life (see page 154)

FOCUS STONE

 Citrine

FIRST RING CRYSTALS

 Black moonstone x 6

SECOND RING CRYSTALS

 Ruby

 Black banded agate

 Herkimer diamond

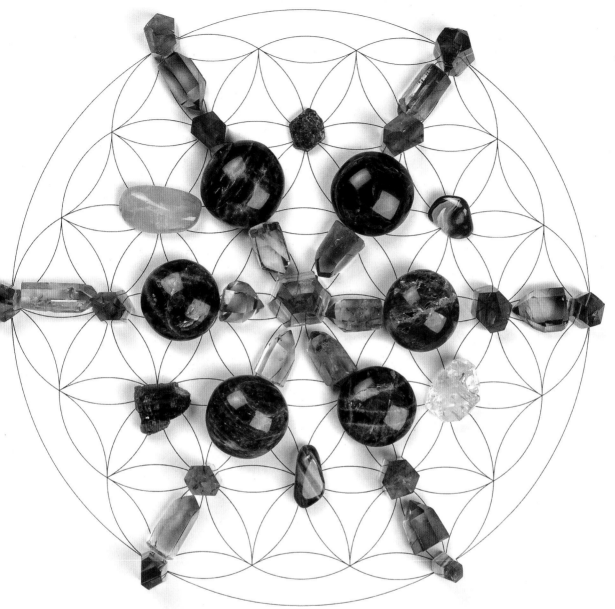

 Tiger's eye

 Pink tourmaline

 Moonstone

AMPLIFIERS

 Citrine x 24

RELATIONSHIPS

If it's friendship or a deeper loving relationship you are seeking, set up this crystal grid. The intention focus is up to you (see Chapter 3). Lasting joyful relationships come from the heart, but also require passion. Whether you're seeking a marriage partner or a lover, or rekindling a current relationship, use this grid to create the spark you need to ignite it.

SACRED GEOMETRY
Flower of life (see page 154)

FOCUS STONE

 Morganite

FIRST RING CRYSTALS

 Rose quartz x 2

 Lapis lazuli x 2

 Citrine x 2

SECOND RING CRYSTALS

 Chrysocolla x 4

 Seraphinite x 4

 Charoite x 14

THIRD RING CRYSTALS

 Fluorite x 18—the more colors the better

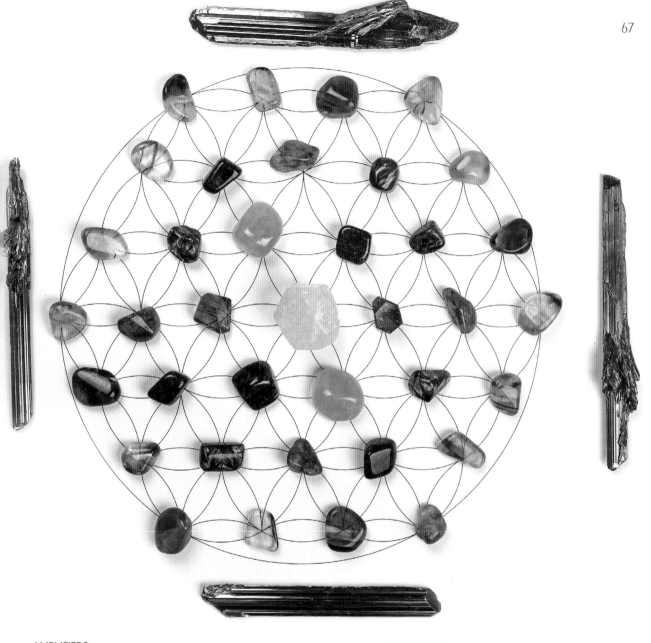

AMPLIFIERS

Stibnite x 4

CRYSTAL TIP

In shamanic tradition, stibnite connects with
the wolf, the path finder of the spirit world,
opening your eyes to new possibilities.

JUST CHILL

We all need a little relaxation in our lives and most of us really need quite a bit more than we actually get. Work this crystal grid to find that quiet moment to bring calmness and serenity, a space where you can be still and relax.

SACRED GEOMETRY
Flower of life
(see page 154)

FOCUS STONE

 Amethyst

FIRST RING CRYSTALS

 Aventurine x 2

 Lapis lazuli x 2

 Imperial topaz x 2

SECOND RING CRYSTALS

 Herkimer diamond x 4

 Smoky quartz x 4

 Jet x 4

AMPLIFIERS

 Amethyst x 18

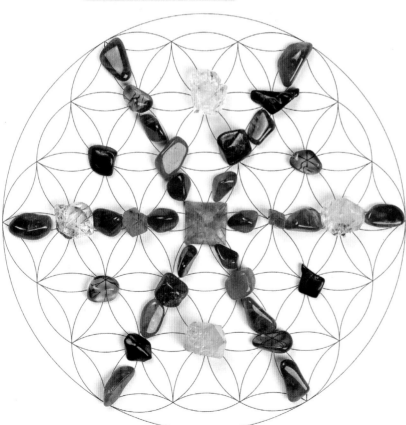

TRAVEL

This grid is deliberately simple because you'll need to take it with you on your travels. It promotes safe travel, allowing you to experience adventures with an energy safety-net. If you are a parent at home, worried about your kids while they're away, set this grid up to send that safety-net energy to your children.

Set the grid up whenever you like—before you leave home or change locations and when you arrive somewhere new are all good times. As a bonus, turquoise and hematite can help suspend the effects of jet-lag.

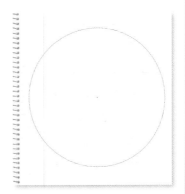

SACRED GEOMETRY
Freeform or a circle
(see page 143)

CRYSTAL TIP

Ideally, carry one aquamarine crystal and, to set in a circle around it, three each of turquoise, hematite, and moonstone.
If you're really tight on space or weight, just take one of each crystal and imagine you are completing a circle with the three crystals surrounding the central aquamarine.

FOCUS STONE

Aquamarine

FIRST RING CRYSTALS

Turquoise × 3

Hematite × 3

Moonstone × 3

COMMUNICATION

Some people are great chatters, while others find it difficult to say anything at all, but good talker or not, if other people don't get your point, you haven't communicated it well. When you really need someone to understand your point of view, set up this grid to help you communicate your thoughts and feelings clearly.

SACRED GEOMETRY
Two interlocking squares forming an eight-pointed star, plus a surrounding circle (see page 152)

FOCUS STONE

Tanzanite

FIRST RING CRYSTALS

Aqua aura x 8

SECOND RING CRYSTALS

Blue lace agate

Aquamarine

Angelite

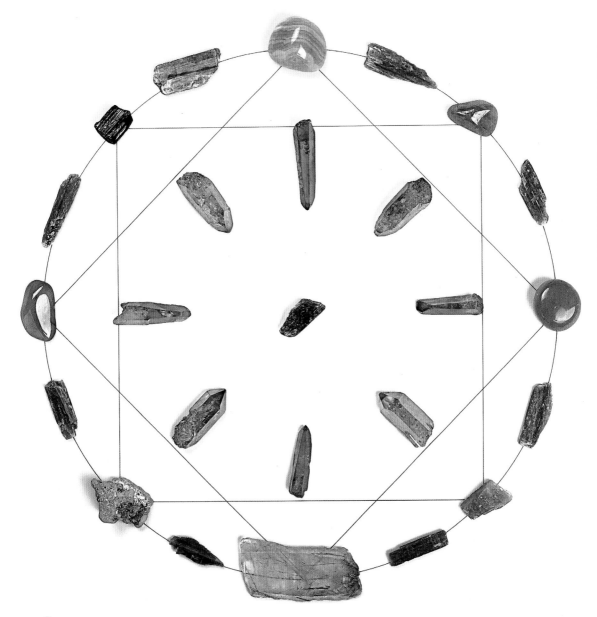

 Blue calcite

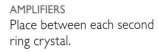 Blue chalcedony

AMPLIFIERS
Place between each second ring crystal.

 Blue quartz

 Blue tourmaline

Kyanite × 8

 Turquoise

DECISIONS

There's an old saying that the decision doesn't matter as long as you make one, and often this is correct. However, for times when it really matters that you make the right choice, create this grid to help you to adopt the best option.

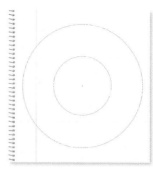

SACRED GEOMETRY
Double circle
(see page 144)

FOCUS STONE

Crocoite

FIRST RING CRYSTALS

Aventurine x 3

Fluorite x 3

SECOND RING CRYSTALS

Muscovite x 4

AMPLIFIERS
Make a central cross or star with the amplifier crystals.

Amethyst x 2

Citrine x 2

Topaz x 2

Stibnite x 2— I only used 1 stibnite crystal as it was long enough to extend to the second ring.

ACHIEVING GOALS

FOCUS STONE

 Sapphire

FIRST RING CRYSTALS

 Citrine

 Red jasper

 Bowenite

 Jade

 Amber

 Tourmaline

 Dioptase

 Howlite

AMPLIFIERS

 Quartz crystals
x 16

It's all very well setting targets in life but you still need to achieve them. This crystal grid is designed to help you order your priorities, set clear achievable goals, focus on the outcome, and move forward in your life.

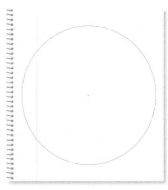

SACRED GEOMETRY
Circle (see page 143)

Right: Awareness, page 82

SPIRITUAL ENHANCEMENT

Above: Dispelling negativity, page 80

Left: Connection, page 90

MAGIC

Magic is defined as something that we can see or sense but cannot explain with today's understanding of science, such as gut feelings, or many complementary therapies. Since there are a lot of holes in science, there's a lot of magic still to be found in the universe!

This grid helps you tune in to the magic and flow with your life path's energy. The natural iridescence of labradorite, the focus stone, reminds us that things are not always as they seem and changes can happen unexpectedly.

SACRED GEOMETRY
Metatron's cube
(see page 155)

FOCUS STONE

Labradorite

FIRST RING CRYSTALS

Quartz x 6

SECOND RING CRYSTALS

Garnet x 3

Tanzanite x 3

ADDITIONAL CRYSTALS

Make a third ring using labradorite (x 12)

AMPLIFIERS

Quartz crystals x 18

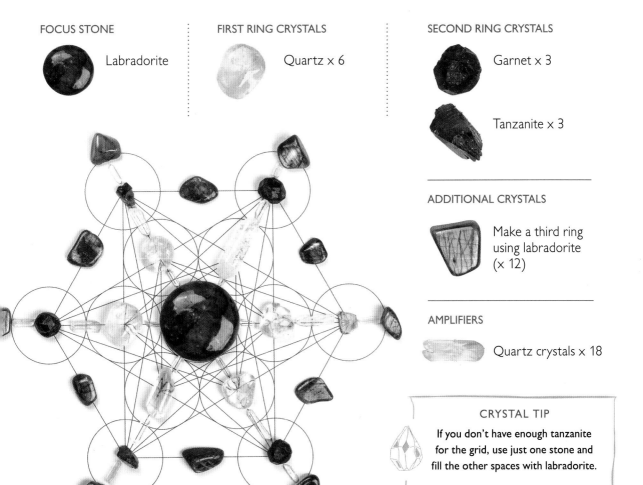

CRYSTAL TIP

If you don't have enough tanzanite for the grid, use just one stone and fill the other spaces with labradorite.

PROTECTION

This grid is deliberately designed without a sacred geometry template so you can create it whenever and wherever it's really needed. Whether you're at home, at work, or away, set this grid up to ward off negativity and danger.

FOCUS STONE

 Tourmaline

FIRST RING CRYSTALS

 Herkimer diamond

 Turquoise

 Black obsidian

 Aqua aura

SECOND RING CRYSTALS

 Lapis lazuli

 Jet

 Sunstone

 Grey banded agate

 Amber

 Spirit quartz

 Angel aura quartz

 Aquamarine

 Red jasper

 Jade

 Stibnite

 Kunzite

THIRD RING CRYSTALS

 As many pyrite crystals as possible—I had 19 crystals

CRYSTAL TIP

Place pyrite crystals against your
walls, on windowsills, and by doors
to quieten noisy neighbors.

DREAMS

Do you want to experience more dreams? Do you want to remember them better? Do you want to use your dream state to influence your life? Do you want to use your dream state to help others? Do you have dreams for your life? If you answer yes to any of these questions, then this crystal grid is for you. Take your time. Set it up once, somewhere near your bed where it won't be disturbed. Reactivate it nightly (see page 30).

Below: The whole grid can also be seen on page 15.

SACRED GEOMETRY
Metatron's cube (see page 155)

FOCUS STONE

Celestite

FIRST RING CRYSTALS

Lapis lazuli × 6

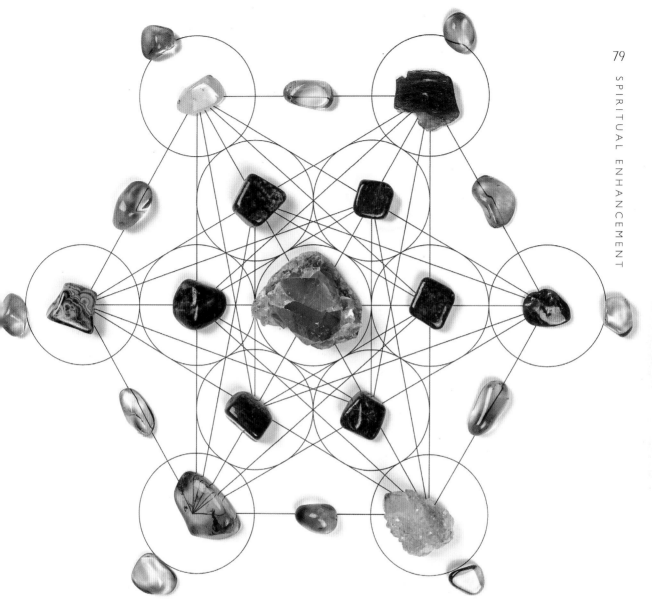

SECOND RING CRYSTALS

 Prehnite

 Moldavite

 Jade

 Spirit quartz

 Amber

 Malachite

ADDITIONAL CRYSTALS

 Make a third ring
with smoky quartz
x 12

DISPELLING NEGATIVITY

Psychic attack! Or simply some unkind words or thoughts from the person you pulled your car out in front of. You sometimes experience jealousy, suspicion, and mistrust of your intentions, even from those who may be close to you. These are all degrees of negativity that can get you down. They appear as dark negative energies in your aura.

When there are too many damaging energies, too much darkness around you, you start to experience detrimental physical and emotional effects. Doctors don't seem to be able to treat these at all well because, of course, they don't have a physical cause even if there are corporal symptoms. Protect yourself from negative energies and dispel them from your life. You'll be amazed how much better you feel!

THIRD RING CRYSTALS

 Imperial topaz x 4

 Aqua aura x 4

 Jade

 Tiger's eye

 Amber

 Apatite

 Kunzite

 Hematite

 Smoky quartz

 Rutilated quartz

 Snowflake obsidian

Turquoise

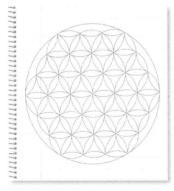

SACRED GEOMETRY
Flower of life (see page 154)

FOCUS STONE

 Black tourmaline

FIRST RING CRYSTALS

 Green tourmaline x 6

SECOND RING CRYSTALS

 Pyrite x 12

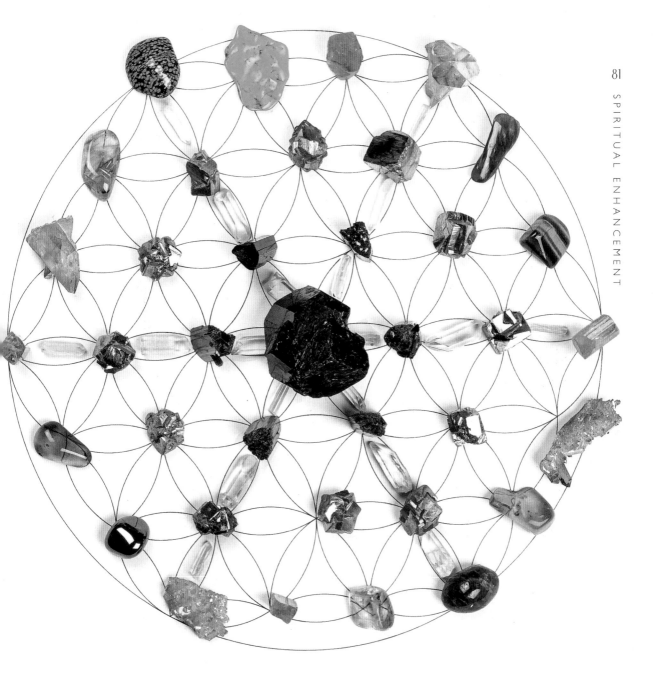

AMPLIFIERS

Quartz crystals
× 18

*Right: Aqua aura is
used in the third
ring of crystals.
The whole grid for
dispelling negativity
can be seen on
page 74.*

AWARENESS

When you want to give your intuition an edge, try this crystal grid. It will give all your psychic abilities a boost, from clairvoyance and clairaudience to sensing auras and crystal-ball reading. Beside that, it will do a lot more for you in everyday life, helping you to be aware of who and what is around you. Is someone close unwell and trying to hide it? How are people feeling about you and themselves? It may even help you to see what someone is thinking about you.

SACRED GEOMETRY
Freeform

FOCUS STONE

 Lapis lazuli

FIRST RING CRYSTALS

Celestite

Aquamarine

Blue quartz

Angelite

SECOND RING CRYSTALS

Phenacite

Lepidolite

Septarian

Magnetite

Alexandrite

Garnet

Citrine

Opal

CRYSTAL TIP

Blue quartz's color is gained from indicolite, blue tourmaline crystals growing through the quartz crystal.

AMPLIFIERS

Kyanite x 16

Right: Blue quartz is used in the first ring of crystals.

HARMONY

When you are in tune with the world around you, everything seems to make sense. Your life becomes easier, energy flows, and new things naturally occur. Think of playing a musical instrument. If you hit a sharp or a flat note, it sounds wrong. In the same way, when you're out of harmony with your world, things seem wrong. Often you can't quite put your finger on it; you just know you don't feel right. Bring the harmony back and life becomes easy again.

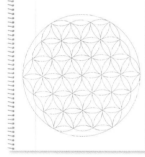

SACRED GEOMETRY
Flower of life
(see page 154)

FOCUS STONE

Calcite—I chose a golden calcite sphere for this crystal grid, but you can choose any variety of calcite that you're drawn toward.

FIRST RING CRYSTALS

Cryolite x 6

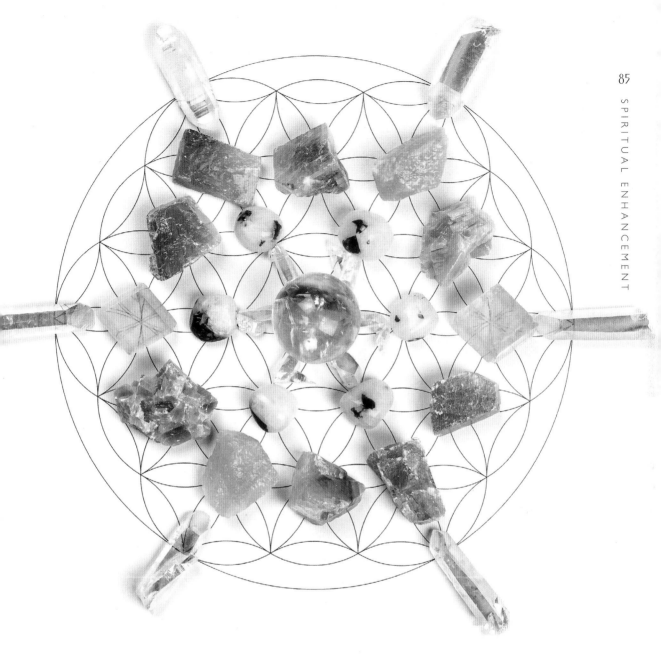

SECOND RING CRYSTALS

Create a ring of calcite crystals in the following colors:

 Honey x 2

Optical x 2

 Green x 2

 Red x 2

 Blue x 2

 Orange x 2

AMPLIFIERS

Angel aura quartz x 12

MEDITATION FOCUS

The purpose of this grid is fulfilled during its creation, because in fact this is a meditation start to finish. It is very important with all grids, but for this one in particular, that you gather everything you need before you commence construction.

SACRED GEOMETRY
Concentric circles
(see page 148)

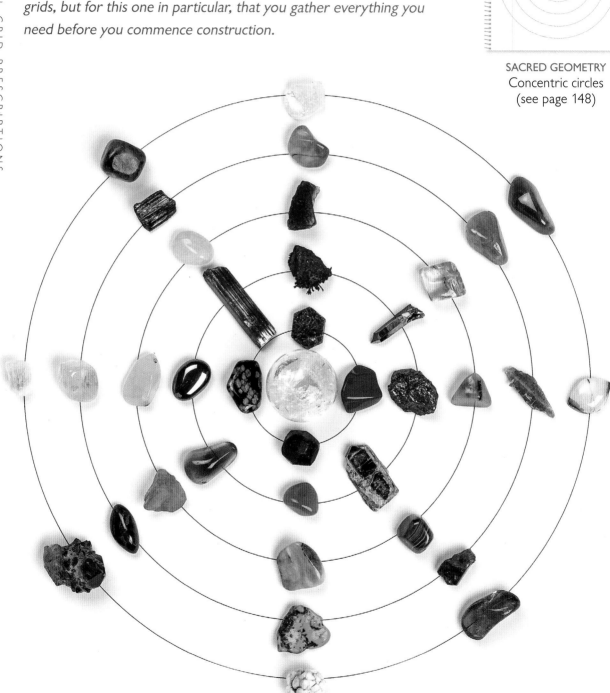

FOCUS STONE

Quartz—a crystal ball, standing point, or crystal cluster is recommended

FIRST RING CRYSTALS

 Ruby

 Red jasper

 Garnet

 Snowflake obsidian

SECOND RING CRYSTALS

 Lodestone

 Titanium quartz

 Chalcopyrite

 Muscovite

 Carnelian

 Smoky quartz

 Hematite

 Stibnite

THIRD RING CRYSTALS

 Moldavite

 Kunzite

 Chrysoprase

 Malachite

 Pink opal

 Peridot

 Prehnite

 Morganite

FOURTH RING CRYSTALS

 Blue fluorite

 Aquamarine

 Kyanite

 Tanzanite

 Turquoise

 Blue apatite

 Topaz

 Tourmaline

CRYSTAL TIP

If you want to add amplifiers to this grid, use quartz crystals.

FIFTH RING CRYSTALS

 Phenacite

 Amethyst

 Opal

 Ametrine

 Magnesite

 Spirit quartz

 Petalite

 Charoite

SPIRITUALITY

This grid can help to enhance any spiritual practice. It doesn't matter if you follow a religion or belief system or not; spirituality is within us all. Open your heart to possibilities and connect to the natural sacred energy that is around everyone. With this crystal grid, you will start to discover how you feel and how you connect with everyone and everything around you.

SACRED GEOMETRY
Metatron's cube (see page 155)

FOCUS STONE

Amethyst

FIRST RING CRYSTALS

Agate × 2

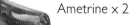

Ametrine × 2

Turquoise × 2

SECOND RING CRYSTALS

Black obsidian × 6

AMPLIFIERS

Quartz crystals × 12

EARTH HEALING

It's too big! What does it matter if I do? No one will notice my little bit of energy ... Well, you're wrong! If everyone spent ten minutes each day sending love to the planet, I'm certain the world would be a little bit better and it would be due to Earth healing. You can help! Send healing thoughts and energy to anywhere in the world that might benefit from it. Whether the focus is a natural or manmade disaster, ongoing environmental issue, or the planet as a whole, Earth healing can help.

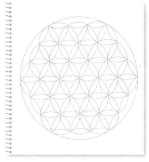

SACRED GEOMETRY
Flower of life (see page 154)

FOCUS STONE

 Chrysocolla sphere

FIRST RING CRYSTALS

 Petrified wood x 6

SECOND RING CRYSTALS

 Larimar x 6

 Turritella agate x 6

THIRD RING CRYSTALS

 Quartz crystals x 18

AMPLIFIERS

 Black tourmaline x 12

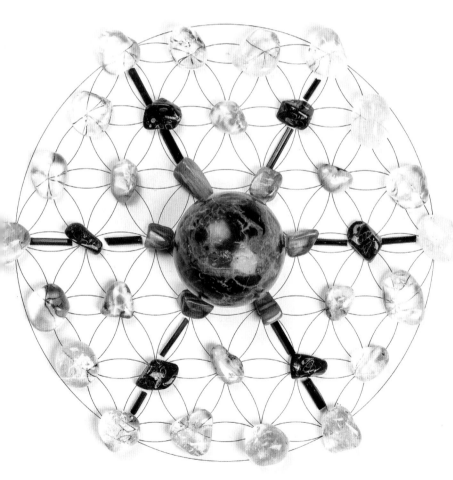

CONNECTION

Sometimes we need a little help from our angels, spirit guides, or guardians, in the form of reassurance, care, universal love, and protection. They are always ready to aid you in any way they can, but first you need to ask for their benevolence. Connect and communicate with them and help these benign beings know what it is that you need assistance with in your life.

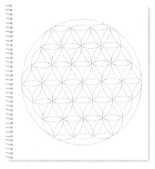

SACRED GEOMETRY
Flower of life
(see page 154)

FOCUS STONE

Angel aura quartz

FIRST RING CRYSTALS

Angelite × 2

Seraphinite × 2

Petalite × 2

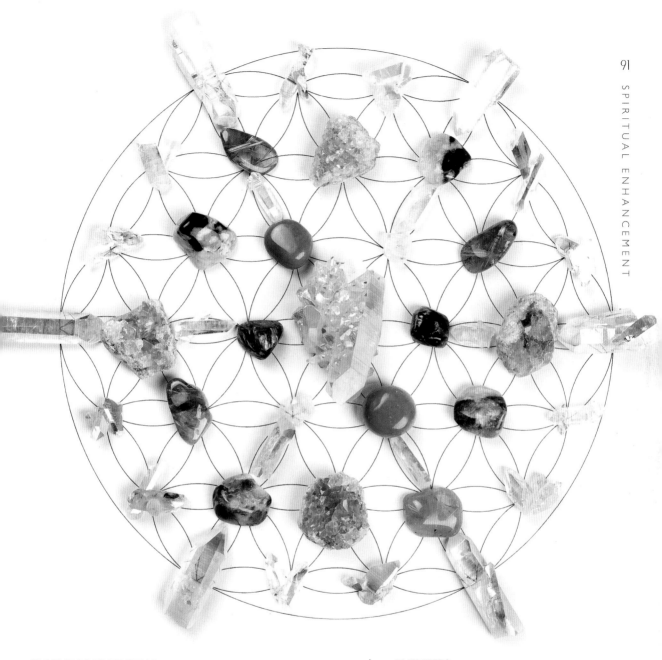

SECOND RING CRYSTALS

 Celestite × 4

 Purple ray opal × 4

AMPLIFIERS

Angel aura quartz × 24

 Rutilated quartz × 4

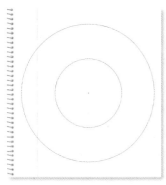

SACRED GEOMETRY
Double circle (see page 144)

FOCUS STONE

Quartz crystal ball

FIRST RING CRYSTALS

Moldavite

Tiger's eye

Ruby

Imperial topaz

SECOND RING CRYSTALS

Ruby x 16

AMPLIFIERS

Quartz crystals x 8

DISTANT HEALING

When you work with a quartz crystal ball, you can send distant healing to anyone. It doesn't matter if you think someone needs it or if that person has just popped into your mind. You may be thinking of friends and relatives on distant shores or just around the corner, or wanting to share your compassion for people you don't know who are trapped or have been affected by disaster. Simply set up this crystal grid to focus and empower your therapeutic thoughts, and send some healing energy their way.

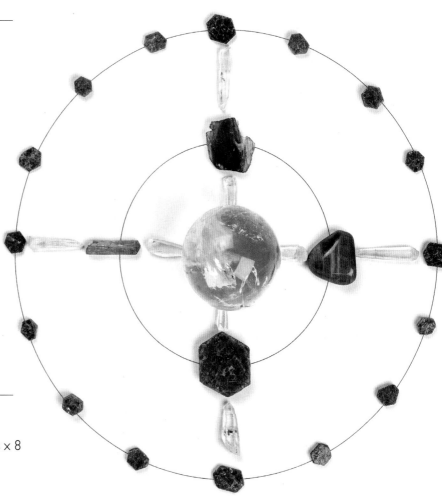

SACRED GEOMETRY
Flower of life (see page 154)

FOCUS STONE

Rose quartz

FIRST RING CRYSTALS

Ruby x 2

Blue quartz x 2

Amethyst x 2

SECOND RING CRYSTALS

Moldavite x 2

Aventurine x 2

Turquoise x 2

AMPLIFIERS

Rose quartz x 18

GRATITUDE AND APPRECIATION

There are many occasions when you want to say "Thank you" to someone, either to appreciate a kind gesture or simply to express gratitude, but for any number of reasons the moment passes. Perhaps the person has left and you haven't been able to convey your feelings. By creating this crystal grid, you can communicate your thoughts to the universe and let the energy associated with your efforts touch those it needs to reach in a way the cosmos directs.

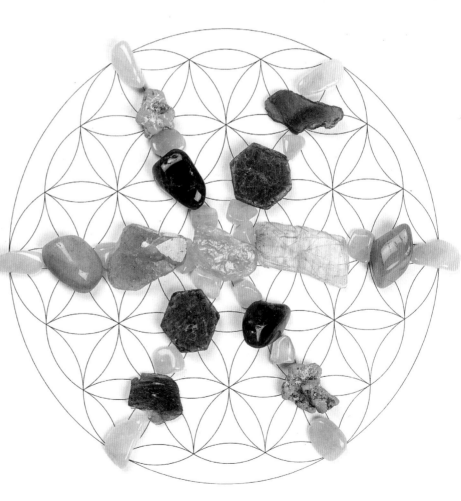

EMOTIONAL CHALLENGES

Above: Grief and loss, page 110

Above: Dispelling fear, page 106

Above: Insight into situations, page 104

FOCUS STONE

Crazy lace agate
(This stone can
have many different
patterns and
shades of color.)

FIRST RING CRYSTALS

Crazy lace agate × 6

SECOND RING CRYSTALS

Moonstone

Dumortierite

Tourmaline

Imperial topaz

Sugilite

Jade

AMPLIFIERS

Tourmaline
× 6

Imperial topaz × 6

Quartz crystal × 6

CONFIDENCE

*The underlying cause of physical
symptoms, such as eczema, psoriasis,
and other skin conditions, or emotional
reactions, such as anxiety and panic
attacks, is often a lack of confidence.
It is also the source of many weight-
related conditions, and a lack of
confidence can stop you fulfilling your
goals and ambitions in life. Apply this
crystal grid to help you overcome such
issues and become all you can be.*

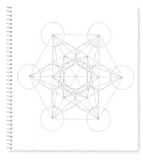

SACRED GEOMETRY
Metatron's cube
(see page 155)

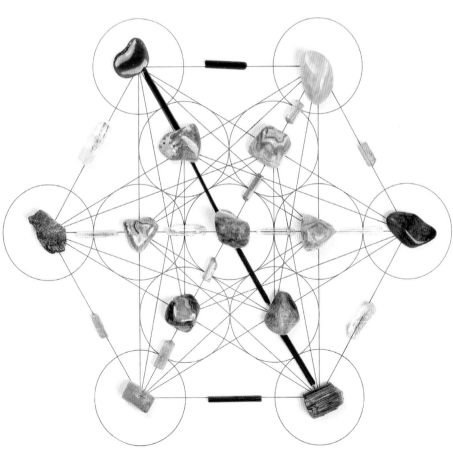

LOVE AND ROMANCE

Whether you're looking for the perfect partner or just want to inject a little romance into your marriage or existing relationship, this is the perfect grid for you.

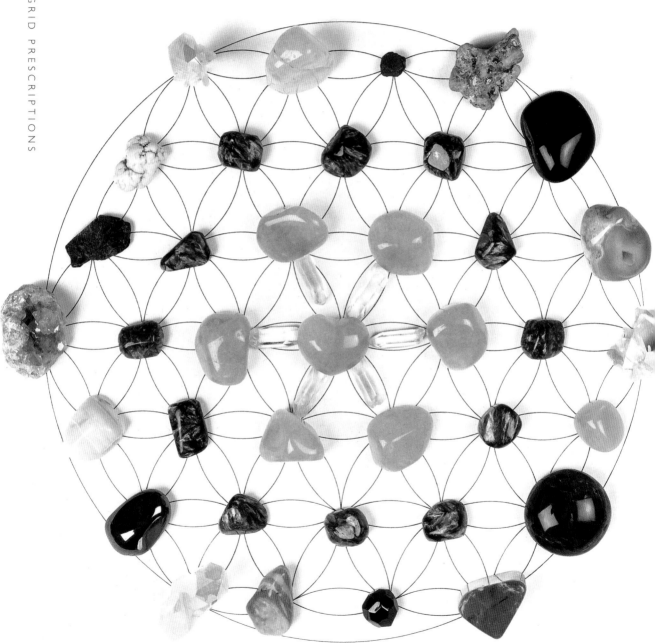

FOCUS STONE

 Rose quartz

FIRST RING CRYSTALS

 Rose quartz x 6

SECOND RING CRYSTALS

 Seraphinite x 12

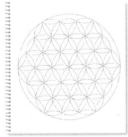

SACRED GEOMETRY
Flower of life
(see page 154)

THIRD RING CRYSTALS

 Morganite

 Magnetite

 Turquoise

 Rainbow obsidian

 Pink banded agate

Bowenite

 Black moonstone

 Kunzite

 Garnet

 Pink opal

 Angel aura quartz x 3

 Hematite

 Manganoan calcite

 Celestite

 Sugilite

 Magnesite

AMPLIFIERS

 Quartz crystals x 6

Right: You may wish to set up your crystal grid on a special copper plate, which can add another dimension of energy.

MENTAL CLARITY

When your mind is filled with fog so you can't even see where you're going inside your head, this crystal grid is the one you need. It brings a gentle breeze through your mind to blow away the fog until you can see clearly again.

SACRED GEOMETRY
Square (see page 150)

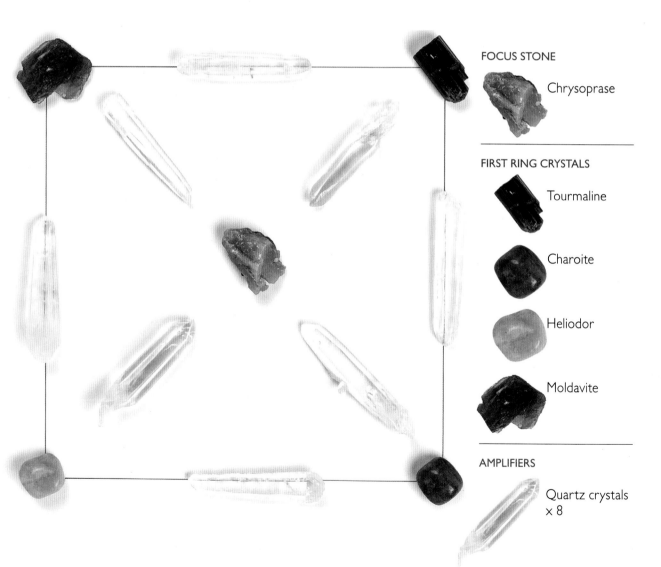

FOCUS STONE

Chrysoprase

FIRST RING CRYSTALS

Tourmaline

Charoite

Heliodor

Moldavite

AMPLIFIERS

Quartz crystals × 8

SACRED GEOMETRY
Triangle within circle
(see page 153)

SELF-LOVE

*If you don't love yourself, like yourself, and value yourself,
it is unlikely others will do so, either. Self-love is selfish, but
look at that word broken down to "self-fish"—to fish for
the self, to search for your inner self. Self-love is a giant leap
along the path of acceptance. Your recognition of your self
is the first step along that path.*

FOCUS STONE

 Morganite

FIRST RING CRYSTALS
(TRIANGLE)

 Eudialyte x 3

 Purple ray opal
x 3

SECOND RING CRYSTALS
(CIRCLE)

 Rose quartz x 9

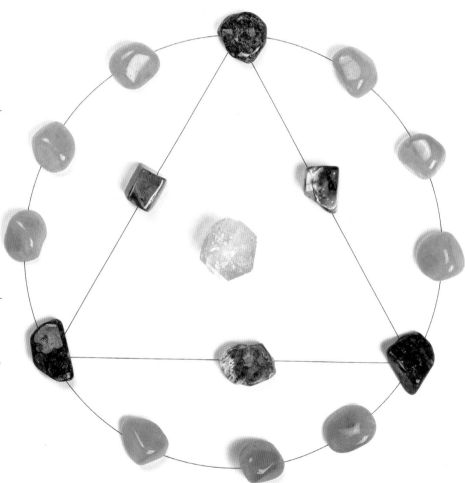

EMOTIONAL STRENGTH

We all have times when we feel emotionally tested, tired, and strained, when we need some help to get by. Different people come up with many different answers, but overall this crystal grid will help. It is designed to bring extra inner-strength to your emotions.

FOCUS STONE

 Orange calcite

FIRST RING CRYSTALS

 Jade

 Dioptase

 Malachite

 Fluorite

 Peridot

 Bowenite

SECOND RING CRYSTALS

 Blue chalcedony

 Rose quartz

 Sapphire

 Cobaltoan calcite

 Garnet

 Rhodochrosite

THIRD RING CRYSTALS

 Muscovite

 Septarian

 Amethyst

 Blue lace agate

 Ametrine

 Alexandrite

ADDITIONAL CRYSTALS

 Make a fourth ring with howlite (x 18)

AMPLIFIERS

Black tourmaline x 18

SACRED GEOMETRY
Flower of life
(see page 154)

DISPELLING ANGER

Anger gets to us. It gets inside you, ties your stomach (or back, neck, hip, gut, heart, or lungs) into knots that strangle your experience of the beauty that is all around you. Let go of it and find freedom from the inner turmoil anger creates with this beautiful crystal grid.

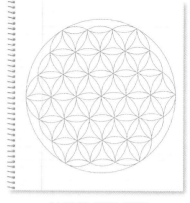

SACRED GEOMETRY
Flower of life (see page 154)

CRYSTAL TIP

Snowflake obsidian frees you from the binds of anger.

FOCUS STONE

Snowflake obsidian

FIRST RING CRYSTALS

Smoky quartz x 6

SECOND RING CRYSTALS

Amethyst x 12

THIRD RING CRYSTALS

Ajoite

Sugilite

Rose quartz

Carnelian

Blue quartz

Howlite

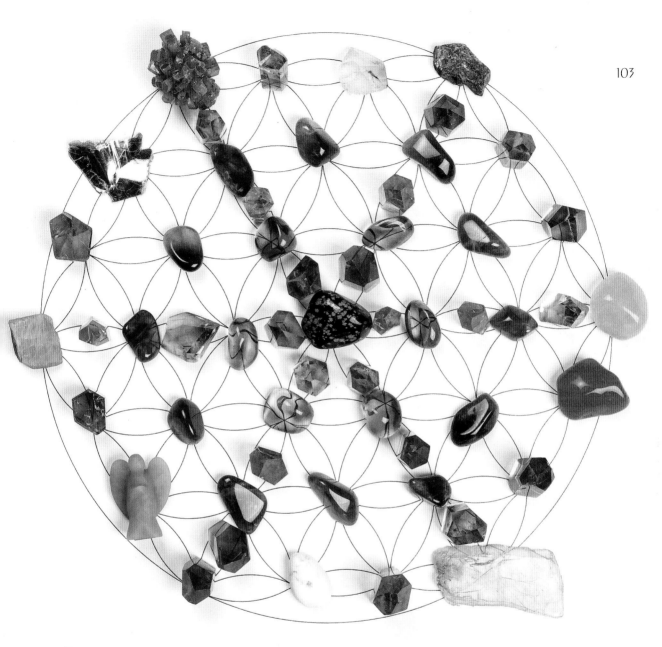

 Angelite

Peridot

 Muscovite

 Aragonite

AMPLIFIERS

 Citrine × 26

INSIGHT INTO SITUATIONS

Understanding what's going on around you is often as important as knowing what is actually happening. This grid is designed to help you to see what's going on behind the scenes and comprehend the reasons, so you can have an insight into events.

SACRED GEOMETRY
Circle (see page 143)

The grid for insight into situations can also be seen on page 43.

FOCUS STONE

Blue quartz

FIRST RING CRYSTALS

Bowenite
× 4

Moonstone
× 4

Fire opal
× 4

AMPLIFIERS

Quartz crystals
× 24

Quartz crystal is sometimes known as the "all singing all dancing" crystal. So, don your party outfit, put on your dancing shoes, and use this crystal grid to bring the fun back into your life!

FOCUS STONE

Quartz crystal cluster

FIRST RING CRYSTALS

Citrine
x 8

SECOND RING CRYSTALS

Rainbow obsidian
x 4

THIRD RING CRYSTALS

Sapphire

Bornite x 2

Blue quartz

FOURTH RING CRYSTALS

Quartz x 4 at the cardinal points

AMPLIFIERS

Quartz crystals
x 12

SACRED GEOMETRY
Freeform

DISPELLING FEAR

Fear can have similar effects to negativity but needs to be treated differently because whereas negativity comes from an external source, fear comes from within you. Your perception of the scale of your fears is important, not what other people think. It doesn't matter how big or small your fears may seem to you, they can all be detrimental to your health, love life, spiritual growth, and prosperity.

SACRED GEOMETRY
Flower of life (see page 154)

FOCUS STONE

Herkimer diamond

FIRST RING CRYSTALS

Rose quartz × 6

SECOND RING CRYSTALS

Carnelian × 4

Sodalite × 4

Seraphinite × 4

Left: Placing your crystal grid on a colored surface can focus your intent. The whole grid can also be seen on page 94.

THIRD RING CRYSTALS

Ajoite

Green calcite

Jet

Spirit quartz

Blue tourmaline

White calcite

Sunstone

Pink tourmaline

Grey banded agate

Black banded agate

Tourmalinated quartz

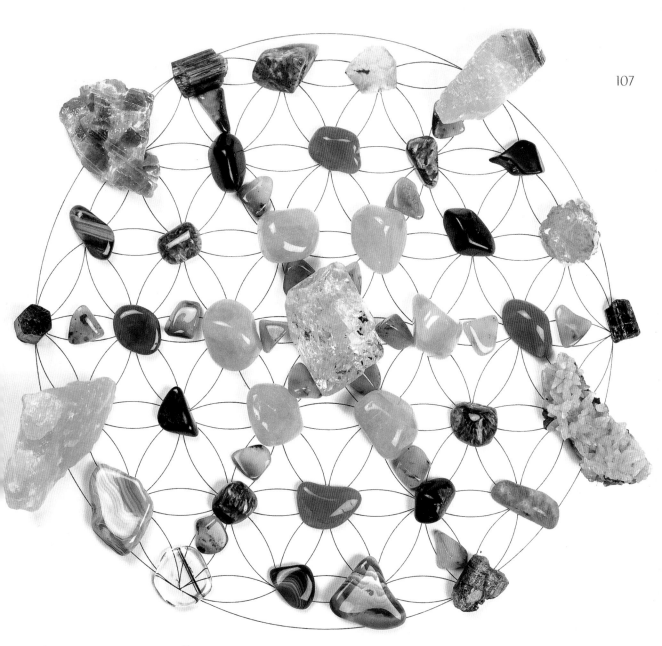

Pink banded agate

Tiger's eye

Green tourmaline

Chrysoprase × 18

Orange calcite

Blue calcite

Crazy lace agate

Black tourmaline

BREAKING PATTERNS

You will have patterns in your life that were learned for a reason and were valuable at the time they started. For example, children who are shouted at every time they speak, or made fun of, will soon learn not to say much. At the time, this makes sense and protects them from fear or shame. However, as these children grow up they become less and less expressive and their learned behavior pattern stops being a benefit and starts to limit and even harm them. Such patterns are best broken and left where they belong—in the past.

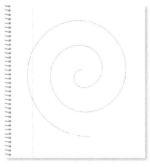

SACRED GEOMETRY
Spiral (see page 151)

FOCUS STONE

Kunzite

FIRST RING CRYSTALS
Continue the spiral from the focus stone with the following crystals.

Moonstone x 12

Alexandrite

Peridot x 4

Charoite x 4

Tourmalinated quartz x 4

SELF-ESTEEM

If you don't feel great about yourself—and it doesn't matter if it's just a blip or you have a longer term lack of self-esteem—you can be much better quickly. Short-term hiccups can be fixed almost instantly as you create this crystal grid; longer term issues take a while and repetition to remedy. This grid will help all cases.

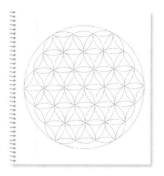

SACRED GEOMETRY
Flower of life
(see page 154)

FOCUS STONE

Rhodonite

FIRST RING CRYSTALS

Citrine x 2

Crazy lace agate x 2

Amethyst x 2

SECOND RING CRYSTALS

Spirit quartz x 4

Alexandrite

Kunzite

THIRD RING CRYSTALS

Sodalite x 18

AMPLIFIERS

Amethyst x 18

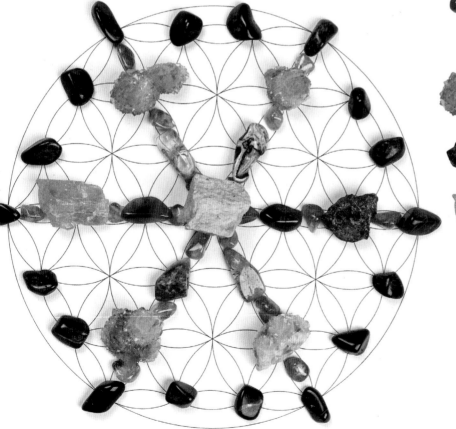

GRIEF AND LOSS

The loss of someone close to you can affect you deeply. Sometimes you don't even realize the effect it is having on you as you carry on your daily tasks with heavy heart and crying soul. On occasion, you just need comfort to come and hold you tightly.

This crystal grid is suitable for any loss, whether of a person, pet, or idea, and as you build it the feeling of a warm hug envelops you. Make this grid and allow it to release any trapped energy from you so you can move gently forward and continue your life.

You can also work with this grid to help others who are in a state of grief to cope with their loss. Sometimes all you can do is send them loving thoughts and this grid will focus and amplify the love and comfort you feel and direct it toward them.

The whole grid can be seen on pages 2 and 94.

SACRED GEOMETRY
Flower of life
(see page 154)

FOCUS STONE

Smoky quartz

FIRST RING CRYSTALS

Apache tear x 2

Amethyst x 2

Bowenite x 2

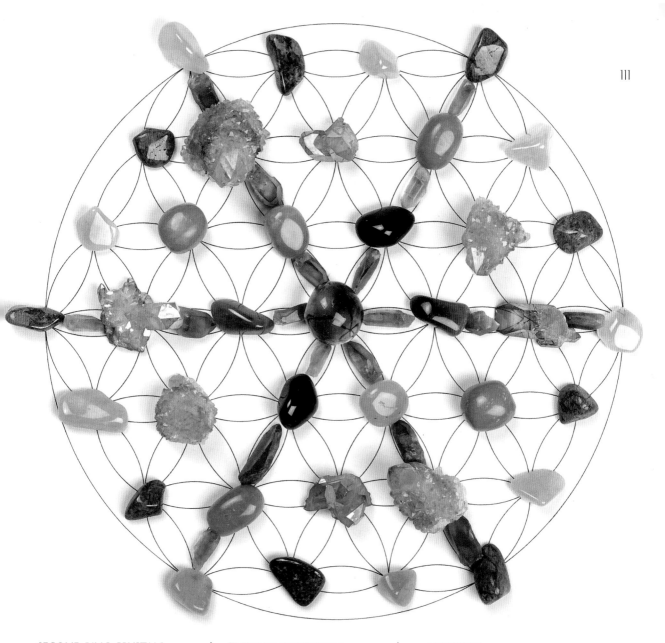

SECOND RING CRYSTALS

 Angelite x 4

 Aqua aura x 4

Spirit quartz x 4

THIRD RING CRYSTALS

 Rose quartz x 9

 Unakite x 9

AMPLIFIERS

 Smoky quartz x 18

ANXIETY

Everyone gets anxious at different times, in different ways, and for different reasons. In fact, anxiety is a uniquely personal experience, so if you feel anxious, you are anxious. Anxiety's effect on each person is different, too. It can lead to anything from mildly increasing stress levels and irritation to full blown, completely disabling, panic attacks. Make setting up this crystal grid and reactivating it (see page 30) part of your daily routine and it will become a powerful friend.

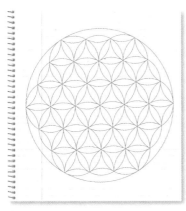

SACRED GEOMETRY
Flower of life (see page 154)

CRYSTAL TIP
It's especially important to keep breathing and stay relaxed when making this crystal grid.

FOCUS STONE

Green calcite

FIRST RING CRYSTALS

Aventurine

Labradorite

Chrysoprase

Green moss agate

Amazonite

Blue quartz

SECOND RING CRYSTALS

Red calcite x 4

Manganoan calcite x 4

Rhodonite x 4

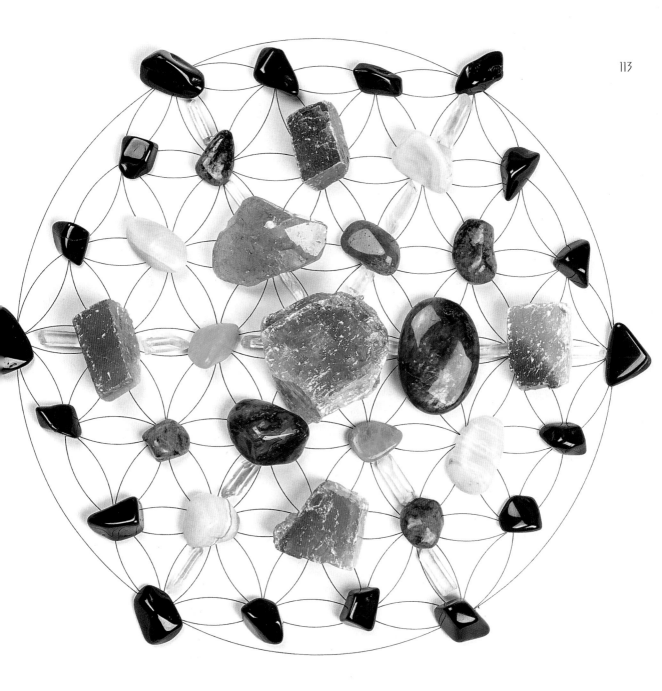

THIRD RING CRYSTALS

Black tourmaline × 18

AMPLIFIERS

Quartz crystals × 18

MENTAL POWER

When you need to block out distractions and focus your mind to bring all your brain's power and potential to the matter in hand, try this crystal grid.

SACRED GEOMETRY
Triangle (see page 146)

FOCUS STONE

Tourmaline

FIRST RING CRYSTALS

Sugilite

Labradorite

Lapis lazuli

Smoky quartz

Celestite

Turquoise

AMPLIFIERS

Imperial topaz x 3

Kyanite x 3

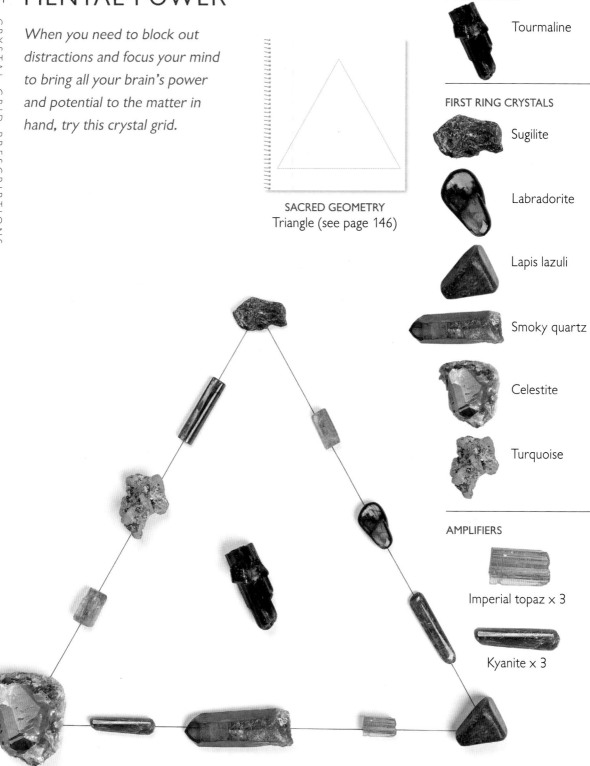

PASSION

Designed to bring more passion into a relationship, this grid can also help any situation that needs more desire to succeed.

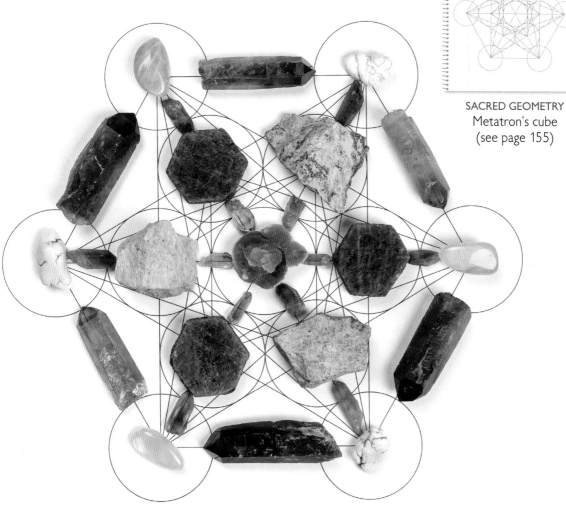

SACRED GEOMETRY
Metatron's cube
(see page 155)

FOCUS STONE	FIRST RING CRYSTALS	SECOND RING CRYSTALS	AMPLIFIERS

Rhodochrosite

 Rhodonite × 3

 Ruby × 3

 Magnesite × 3

 Moonstone × 3

Smoky quartz × 18

PHYSICAL
HEALING

Above: Strength and physical ability, see opposite

STRENGTH AND PHYSICAL ABILITY

This grid has several aims, all to do with accessing and applying your physical energy. Designed to give you the edge over the competition in any sport, physical competition, or personal challenge, it is built on the sacred geometry of the triangle, which is the strongest shape in nature.

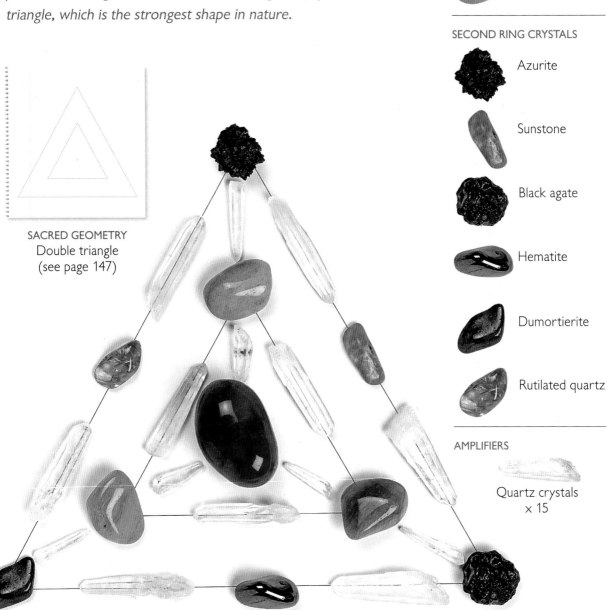

SACRED GEOMETRY
Double triangle
(see page 147)

FOCUS STONE
Carnelian

FIRST RING CRYSTALS
Aventurine x 3

SECOND RING CRYSTALS
Azurite

Sunstone

Black agate

Hematite

Dumortierite

Rutilated quartz

AMPLIFIERS
Quartz crystals
x 15

SPORTS

This grid is great to set up well before any sporting activity or anything physically challenging you might need to do. Set your pyrite crystal in the center. To the north, place howlite; carnelian in the west; to the south, aventurine; to the east, agate. Essentially you are following the instructions for the medicine wheel on page 20, using these crystals instead of tourmaline.

SACRED GEOMETRY
Square set in
compass directions
(see page 150)

FOCUS STONE

Pyrite

FIRST RING CRYSTALS

Howlite

Carnelian

Aventurine

Agate

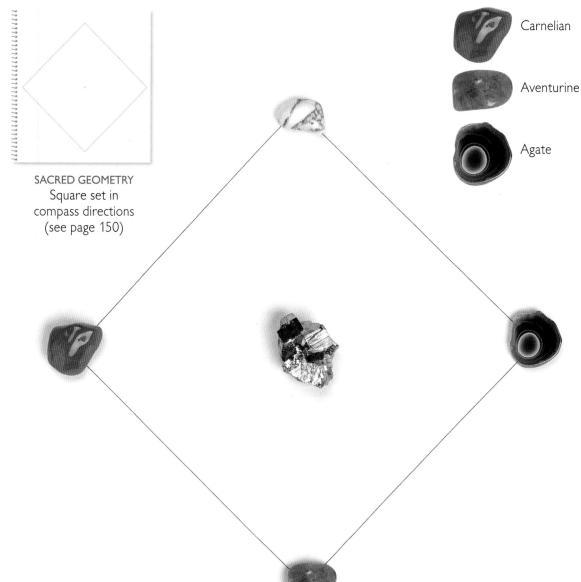

HEALTH AND HEALING

This grid is designed as a general tonic for health and as a focus for any specific healing needs. It will help you to focus on staying well, especially in stressful times, and it can also help you to direct your healing energy where you need it within your body.

FOCUS STONE

Quartz crystal ball

FIRST RING CRYSTALS

Rose quartz x 6

SECOND RING CRYSTALS

Super seven x 6

Turquoise x 6

ADDITIONAL CRYSTALS

Select any other crystals that might aid the specific illness or condition (see Chapter 5) to go around the outside of the crystal grid.

SACRED GEOMETRY
Metatron's cube
(see page 155)

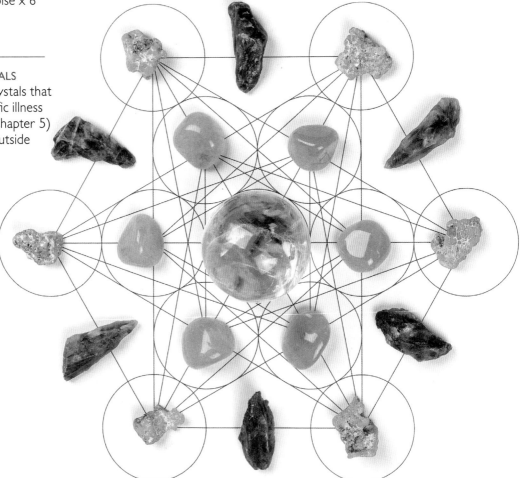

SLEEP

Whether your problem is long-term insomnia or being stressed and not sleeping well, set up this crystal grid and start experiencing a better night's rest. Create it next to your bed every night for two weeks in order to achieve the long-term benefits it can bring.

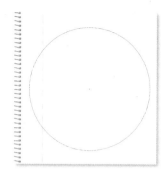

SACRED GEOMETRY
Circle (see page 143)

FOCUS STONE

Malachite

FIRST RING CRYSTALS

Lapis lazuli × 2

Muscovite × 2

Manganoan calcite × 2

ADDITIONAL CRYSTALS

Malachite in between each pair of first ring crystals (× 6)

AMPLIFIERS

Quartz crystals × 18

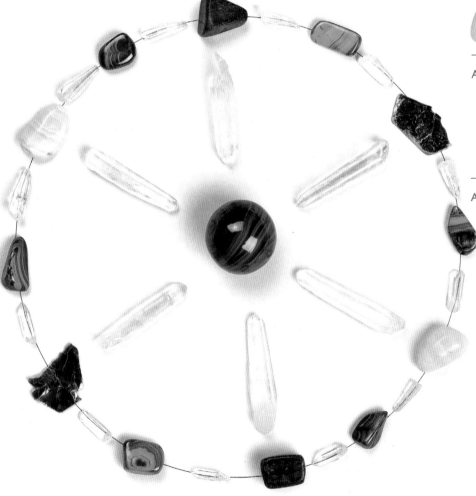

FOCUS STONE

Rose quartz

FIRST RING CRYSTALS

Emerald

Unakite

Tektite

Chrysoprase

Pink
tourmaline

Bowenite

SECOND RING CRYSTALS

Moonstone x 4

Jade x 4

Spirit quartz
x 4

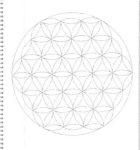

SACRED GEOMETRY
Flower of life
(see page 154)

FERTILITY

Sometimes there's no physical reason why someone cannot conceive; it just doesn't seem to happen. In this scenario, create this grid together with your partner to intertwine your energies, and to focus your intent and your love. You can make the grid as big as you like.

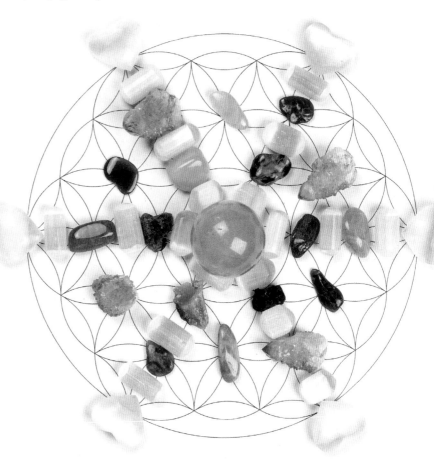

THIRD RING CRYSTALS

Selenite x 6
(I used heart-shaped
selenite crystals)

AMPLIFIERS

Selenite x 18

CHAPTER 5

CRYSTAL INDEX

FIND CRYSTALS BY COLOR

Every crystal has its own natural energy, which can be harnessed within your crystal grid. Whether it is for healing or creating positive changes in your life there are suitable crystals for every situation. This is a quick color-coded guide to a selection of powerful crystals and their energy benefits when employed inside a crystal grid.

RED

GARNET

Dodecahedral and trapezohedral crystals and combinations, masses, and layered plates. Colors and varieties include red, pink (known as eudialyte), pink/red (rhodolite), green (grossularite), emerald green (uvarovite), black (melanite), orange (spessartine), red/purple (almandine), greenish yellow (andradite), and yellow and brown (hessonite).
BRINGS: vitality to any situation
CHAKRA: heart
HEALING FOCUS: blood, enhanced blood flow to damaged tissue, removal of toxins
CRYSTAL GRID KEYWORDS: cleansing, courage, strength, drive, happiness, creativity, abundance, change, awareness, vitality, magic, spiritual devotion, flow, aura, emotional trauma, chaos, disruption, structure.

RUBY

Red variety of corundum, forming tabular hexagonal crystals.
BRINGS: spiritual love
CHAKRA: heart
HEALING FOCUS: blood, heart, menstrual cycle
CRYSTAL GRID KEYWORDS: abundance, balance, energy, longevity, mind focus, passion, will to live, spiritual wisdom, health, wealth, knowledge, protection, distress, relief of suffering, decisions, lightning strikes of inspiration and love, dreams, meditation, change, creativity, rebirth, new beginnings, distant healing, spirit guides.

RED JASPER

A variety of quartz, forming rocks and colored red by iron oxide inclusion.
BRINGS: direction
CHAKRA: base
HEALING FOCUS: preventing illness
CRYSTAL GRID KEYWORDS: protection, rebirth, new ideas, astral travel, meditation, survival instinct, dream recall.

ORANGE

CARNELIAN

Variety of chalcedony, forming orange pebbles. It can also be found in red, pink, and brown.
BRINGS: energy and an understanding of the links between dis-ease and emotions so you can deal with the emotions and prevent disease.
CHAKRA: sacral
HEALING FOCUS: infection
CRYSTAL GRID KEYWORDS: appetite, anger, envy, fear, rage, sorrow, focus, balance, courage, compassion, confusion, digestion, vitality, personal power, jealousy, memory, speech, voice, self-esteem, structure, a feel-better stone, study, inspiration, connection to spirit, links, meditation, inquisitiveness, apathy, performance, kick up the backside!

CROCOITE

Prismatic orange crystals, masses, and aggregates.
BRINGS: massive change!
CHAKRA: sacral
HEALING FOCUS: immense stress, reproductive system
CRYSTAL GRID KEYWORDS: intuition, creativity, sexuality, changes (especially the big ones!), death, distress, "the divorce stone," emotions, letting go, release.

SUNSTONE

Type of oligoclase, which is a variety of the feldspar mineral plagioclase. Goethite and hematite are common inclusions, which give the sparkly (sun) effect.
BRINGS: revitalization
CHAKRA: crown
HEALING FOCUS: hands and feet
CRYSTAL GRID KEYWORDS: fear, stress, vitality, strength, energy, abundance, longevity, spirit guides, protection.

YELLOW

CITRINE

A yellow, golden, or lemon variety of quartz, forming hexagonal crystals and crystal clusters. The color of natural citrine is due to heat from the earth's activity. Enhanced citrine is heated quartz, often amethyst.
BRINGS: abundance to any situation
CHAKRA: solar plexus
HEALING FOCUS: digestive system, recovery after surgery or injury

CRYSTAL GRID KEYWORDS: abundance, success, happiness, ideas, creativity, writing, money, finance, job, career, making decisions and taking responsibility, inspiration, teaching, learning, studying, problem-solving, new beginnings, relationships, self-esteem, anger, yin/yang balance, bravery, strength, confidence, logic, memory, concentration, adaptability, awareness, energy, release of toxic emotions, welcoming.

COPPER

Metal forming free-form shapes, dendrites, plates, and rhombohedral crystals.
BRINGS: a boost of chi and flow of energy
CHAKRA: sacral
HEALING FOCUS: joints
CRYSTAL GRID KEYWORDS: vitality, energy, luck, flexibility, flow, detox, movement, transforming, transmuting.

HELIODOR

Yellow or golden variety of beryl, forming hexagonal prismatic crystals with flat or occasionally small pyramidal terminations. Heliodor is sometimes known as golden aquamarine.
BRINGS: mental equilibrium
CHAKRA: solar plexus, crown
HEALING FOCUS: liver
CRYSTAL GRID KEYWORDS: mind, communication, protection (especially when you are away from your house, car, family), finding answers, compassion, mental balance.

IMPERIAL TOPAZ

Golden prismatic crystals and alluvial pebbles.
BRINGS: universal connection to everything and feeling of oneness
CHAKRA: solar plexus, crown
HEALING FOCUS: stress-related conditions
CRYSTAL GRID KEYWORDS: connection, physical attraction, mental energy, creativity, thoughts, ideas, goals, success, protection, relaxation, meditation, inspiration, de-stress, detail.

AMBER

Fossilized resin from prehistoric trees that may have inclusions of animal and/or plant material. Colors include yellow, orange, brown, blue, and green (artificial).
BRINGS: memories
CHAKRA: solar plexus
HEALING FOCUS: the past
CRYSTAL GRID KEYWORDS: past, memory, intellect, making choices, purification, good luck, protection, dreams, goals, ideals, marriage, cleansing, detox, yin/yang balance, emotional blockage, calming, stress relief, communication especially of ideas, letting go.

TIGER'S EYE

A member of the quartz family. Tiger's eye shows chatoyancy, an optical reflectance effect giving a shimmer to the stone as you move it in the light, due to its fibrous structure. It is similar to, but not the same as, the cat's eye effect. Colors include gold, yellow, brown, blue (hawk's eye), and red (falcon's eye).
BRINGS: courage
CHAKRA: solar plexus
HEALING FOCUS: digestion
CRYSTAL GRID KEYWORDS: "go for it!", intuition, strength, new beginnings, success, wealth, distant healing, sharpening of the mind, investigation, science, openness, open-mindedness, abundance, money, wealth, yin/yang balance, ideas, calmness, dispelling fear, carefree, uplifting, spontaneity, removal of self-sabotaging behaviors, grounding.

BUMBLE BEE JASPER

Yellow, black, and gray banding that often resembles a bumble bee. Some people refer to this as agate because of the swirling patterns that may also be present. Contains sulfur and arsenic—**wash your hands before eating anything**.
BRINGS: self-esteem
CHAKRA: sacral, solar plexus
HEALING FOCUS: physical vitality, allergies
CRYSTAL GRID KEYWORDS: work, busy-ness, buzz, joint effort, teamwork, sharing, sweetness, sting, vitality, energy, abundance, family.

ALEXANDRITE

Green variety of chrysoberyl showing color change to red under artificial light. Usually small masses and, rarely, crystals.
BRINGS: emotional and mental balance
CHAKRA: heart
HEALING FOCUS: nerve damage, dementia
CRYSTAL GRID KEYWORDS: past issues, past lives, rebirth, youthfulness, creativity, awareness, self-esteem, good fortune.

AVENTURINE

Quartz variety with mica inclusions, giving a speckled or sparkly effect. Commonly green; other colors include blue, white, red/peach, and brown.
BRINGS: success
CHAKRA: heart
HEALING FOCUS: muscles
CRYSTAL GRID KEYWORDS: reactions, speed, calming, protecting and soothing emotions, relaxing, exams, creativity, motivation, yin/yang, decisions, leadership, spirit guides, "energy vampires."

CHRYSOCOLLA

Layers, masses, botryoidal structures, and druses. The translucent gemmy form of chrysocolla is called gem silica. Color is blue/green.
BRINGS: a speeding up of the effects of other crystals
CHAKRA: heart
HEALING FOCUS: menstrual cycle, lunar cycles, behavioral cycles
CRYSTAL GRID KEYWORDS: creativity, digestion of ideas, movement, freedom, phobias, sexuality, tension, feel better, pregnancy, babies, broken heart, Earth healing, easing stressful situations, releasing negative emotions, revitalizing relationships, restful sleep, breath.

SERAPHINITE/ CLINOCHLORE

Chlorite mineral, forms green and white, colorless, and yellow masses and occasional crystals.
BRINGS: nurture
CHAKRA: heart
HEALING FOCUS: critical conditions
CRYSTAL GRID KEYWORDS: relationships, broken heart, fear of the unknown, connection with angels and guardians, nurture, spiritual love.

EMERALD

Green gem variety of beryl, forming hexagonal prismatic crystals with flat or occasionally small pyramidal terminations.
BRINGS: happiness
CHAKRA: heart
HEALING FOCUS: liver
CRYSTAL GRID KEYWORDS: balance, structure, seeing clearly, fertility, growth, heart and soul, honesty, memory, patience, vitality.

AJOITE

Usually found as green phantoms in quartz crystals and, rarely, as a druse.
BRINGS: love to replace fear
CHAKRA: heart
HEALING FOCUS: restoring youthfulness
CRYSTAL GRID KEYWORDS: speaking your truth, calming, self-love, delight, confidence, tolerance, creativity, spirit contact.

AMAZONITE

Usually opaque variety of microcline (variety of feldspar), forming crystals and masses. Color varies from yellow/green to blue/green.
BRINGS: calm mind
CHAKRA: heart
HEALING FOCUS: nervous system
CRYSTAL GRID KEYWORDS: soothing, calming, nervousness, stress, aura, creativity, troubled mind, a feel-better stone.

DIOPTASE

Brilliant emerald green prismatic crystals and masses.
BRINGS: understanding of the cause of dis-ease
CHAKRA: all, especially heart
HEALING FOCUS: stomach
CRYSTAL GRID KEYWORDS: abundance, defense, balance, yin/yang, circulation, release, emotional stability, inner strength, vitality, living in the moment, healthy babies, change, renewal of goals, digesting ideas, ideals, past lives, soothing, feeding.

TREE AGATE

Massive opaque variety of agate with green and white patterns resembling foliage.
BRINGS: the ability to see the beauty in everything
CHAKRA: heart
HEALING FOCUS: shock
CRYSTAL GRID KEYWORDS: very calming, comfort, ego, spiritual growth, plants, gardens, "green fingers," gentle healing.

MALACHITE

Crystalline aggregates, druses, botryoidal structures, and clusters of radiating fibrous crystals. Single prismatic crystals are rare. More common are malachite pseudomorphs of azurite, which produce a tabbier crystal. Color is green, often of various shades and with black bands.
BRINGS: healing
CHAKRA: heart
HEALING FOCUS: heart, emotions
CRYSTAL GRID KEYWORDS: emotional balance, calming, uplifting, restful sleep, dream interpretation, clear sight, endurance, heart and soul, different views of a situation, meditation, regeneration, new beginnings.

PREHNITE

Massive botryoidal and globular structures, layered plates, tabular and prismatic crystals. Colors are green, yellow, white, and brown.
BRINGS: an ability to find your own true spiritual path through life
CHAKRA: heart and brow
HEALING FOCUS: kidneys
CRYSTAL GRID KEYWORDS: prophesy, visualization, meditation, calmness, tranquility, letting go, dreams, dream recall, divination, inspiration, flow.

CHRYSOPRASE

Green or yellow (lemon) variety of chalcedony.
BRINGS: clarity of thought and mind, helping you to find and accept the root cause of your stress
CHAKRA: heart and brow
HEALING FOCUS: mental health
CRYSTAL GRID KEYWORDS: seeing through the fog in your mind, calmness, depression, confidence, balance, breaking patterns, stress, meditation, humility, modesty, non-judgmental, acceptance of others, self-acceptance, broken heart, dexterity, fertility, sexuality, a feel-better stone.

PERIDOT

Small green prismatic crystals and masses. Other colors include red, brown, and yellow. Peridot is also known as chrysolite and olivine.
BRINGS: peace
CHAKRA: heart
HEALING FOCUS: effects of cancer
CRYSTAL GRID KEYWORDS: balance acidity, addictions, detox, digestion of ideas, contentment, emotional blockages, breakthrough, action, motivation, stress, a feel-better stone, weight gain, behavior patterns and cycles, protection from outside influences, ego, happiness, enlightenment, meditation, general physical health, childbirth, beginning, start, refresh, rebirth.

GREEN MOSS AGATE

Massive transparent or translucent green, white, and clear moss-like patterned variety of agate; also comes in red, yellow, brown, black, and blue varieties.
BRINGS: growth
CHAKRA: heart
HEALING FOCUS: digestion
CRYSTAL GRID KEYWORDS: calmness, stress, release of tension, cleansing, detox, growth of new ideas, creativity, wealth, abundance, release of trapped emotions, positivity.

MOLDAVITE

Green tektite originally created from meteorite impact melting the earth's surface and itself. Moldavite is the resulting re-formed natural glass material, part earth, part space.
BRINGS: the possibility of the possible
CHAKRA: brow
HEALING FOCUS: physical and mental balance
CRYSTAL GRID KEYWORDS: possibilities, new possibilities, new experiences, new opportunities, altered mind states, meditation, dreams, hypnosis, discovery, travel.

BOWENITE

Massive fine-granular green rock variety of antigorite; also known as new jade.
BRINGS: freedom to travel your path
CHAKRA: heart
HEALING FOCUS: cholesterol
CRYSTAL GRID KEYWORDS: love, friendship, connection to ancestors, grief, success in business, abundance, personal goals and ambitions, making a clean break from the past, release of past traumas, soul mate, removing blocks you put in your own way, change, adventure, meditation, answers, insight, joy, happiness, fertility, protection from enemies.

JADE

Massive form in many colors including green, orange, brown, blue, cream, white, lavender, red, gray, and black. Types of jade include jadeite and nephrite.
BRINGS: wisdom
CHAKRA: heart
HEALING FOCUS: female reproductive system including fallopian tubes, fertility, ovaries, menstrual cycle, menstruation, period pains, PMT, PMS, vagina, and womb
CRYSTAL GRID KEYWORDS: protection from accidents, balance, confidence, courage, child's first stone, emotional balance, grounding, justice, longevity, modesty, negativity, wisdom, compassion, dreams, goals, ideals, connection to ancient civilizations and wisdom, protection, peace and inner peace, spirit worlds, problem-solving, finding answers.

PINK BANDED AGATE

Agate variety with pink, white, and possibly gray banding and patterns.
BRINGS: femininity
CHAKRA: heart and sacral
HEALING FOCUS: nervous system
CRYSTAL GRID KEYWORDS: pleasure, softness, mystery, creativity, nurture, solutions, problem-solving, attention to detail, universal love, seeing the whole picture, detox, contentment, stress.

EUDIALYTE

Variety of pink garnet often intermingled with other minerals, such as tourmaline and calcite.
BRINGS: an open heart
CHAKRA: heart
HEALING FOCUS: eye disorders
CRYSTAL GRID KEYWORDS: open heart, emotional release, connection, past, childhood, past lives, ancestors, self-love, forgiveness, change, variety.

KUNZITE

Pink variety of spodumene, forming flattened prismatic crystals, vertically striated. Other colors include lilac, blue, green (hiddenite), yellow, and clear (spodumene); sometimes has bi- or tri-colored crystals.
BRINGS: control
CHAKRA: heart
HEALING FOCUS: stress-related conditions
CRYSTAL GRID KEYWORDS: desire, belief, behavior patterns, addiction, smoking cessation, calm, hope, glamour, sexuality, self-esteem, youthfulness, expression, love, flow, removal of obstacles, negativity in the environment, protection, shield, centering, meditation, a feel-better stone, maturity, energy blocks.

MANGANOAN CALCITE

Massive with pink and white bands.
BRINGS: calmness
CHAKRA: heart
HEALING FOCUS: trauma
CRYSTAL GRID KEYWORDS: love, peacefulness, restfulness, calmness, sleep, dreams, stillness, emotion, feeling.

MORGANITE

Pink variety of beryl, forming hexagonal prismatic crystals with flat or occasionally small pyramidal terminations.
BRINGS: love
CHAKRA: heart
HEALING FOCUS: fills the space left in the heart by loss
CRYSTAL GRID KEYWORDS: relationships, death, loss, bereavement, love, open-mindedness, spirit guides, calmness, meditation, wisdom, ceremony, seeing things from a different perspective, clear thought, time saving, physical healing.

PINK OPAL

Pink masses sometimes showing iridescence.
BRINGS: a fresh start
CHAKRA: heart
HEALING FOCUS: heart and lungs
CRYSTAL GRID KEYWORDS: rebirth, renewal, love, behavior patterns, calm, clears the mind allowing space to think, spiritual awakening, self-healing, starting, meditation, mind, soothing, new beginnings.

RHODOCHROSITE

Masses, druses, botryoidal structures, and, rarely, small rhombohedral crystals. Colors range from pale pink to deep red, yellow, orange, and brown. The massive material commonly displays pink and white banding when polished.
BRINGS: passion
CHAKRA: heart
HEALING FOCUS: 21st-century stress
CRYSTAL GRID KEYWORDS: flow, circulation, confidence, courage, strength, strong heart, memory, past, calming, wisdom, babies, music, writing, sex, yin/yang.

RHODONITE

Pink or red tabular crystals and masses. Rhodonite is also found in green, yellow, and black, usually with veined inclusions of manganese giving black lines through the structure.
BRINGS: grounding, the feeling of love in the physical world
CHAKRA: heart
HEALING FOCUS: mental balance
CRYSTAL GRID KEYWORDS: balance, peacefulness, calming, clarity, memory, time, self-esteem, sensitivity, music, yin/yang, unconditional spiritual love, consistency, attention to detail, communication.

ROSE QUARTZ

Pink crystalline masses and, rarely, small hexagonal crystals.
BRINGS: love
CHAKRA: heart
HEALING FOCUS: emotions—the equivalent of a spa day for the emotions
CRYSTAL GRID KEYWORDS: love, relationships, romance, sexuality, sex drive, fertility, breakthrough, good fortune, luck, youthfulness, calmness, kindness, peace, pleasure, happiness, relaxation, contentedness, confidence, forgiveness, innocence, grief, skill, ability, talent, calming, trusting, childhood, emotion, stillness, creativity, art, music, writing, imagination, detox.

Left: Rose quartz is like a spa day for your emotions. Keep ruby near your rose quartz to bring a blissful state of spiritual love.

CHALCOPYRITE

Tetrahedral crystals with sphenoid faces, octahedral crystals, and masses. Colors include gold, blue, green, and purple, usually brightly iridescent. Color comes from the natural oxidation of the surface. Scratching may remove bright colors, leaving a gray rock!
BRINGS: balance of color in energy
CHAKRA: crown
HEALING FOCUS: side effects of medication
CRYSTAL GRID KEYWORDS: perception, psychic ability, connection, connection to the universe, removal of energy blocks, detox, meditation, endurance, flow of chi, growth.

TITANIUM QUARTZ

Quartz crystal bonded with titanium and niobium.
BRINGS: help in finding your own true path through life
CHAKRA: crown, all
HEALING FOCUS: fluids, dehydration, water retention
CRYSTAL GRID KEYWORDS: centering, openness, other points of view, meditation, energy flow, change, career, decisions, sensing, auras, a feel-better crystal, direction, possibilities.

OPAL

Masses in a multitude of colors including white (common opal), pink, black, beige, blue, yellow, brown, orange, red, green, and purple, sometimes showing iridescence (fire) in various colors. Colors are caused by the diffraction of light within the crystalline structure, and opal varieties are often named for the color, such as pink opal and black opal. Common opal does not have a diffraction grating in its structure and so shows no color.
BRINGS: good and bad characteristics to the surface—the bad ones come out so you can deal with them
CHAKRA: heart, throat, crown
HEALING FOCUS: eyes
CRYSTAL GRID KEYWORDS: creativity, inspiration, imagination, permission, memory, psychic abilities, shamanic visions, detox, vision, childbirth, flow, passion.

LABRADORITE

Massive plagioclase feldspar with albite, occasionally forming tabular crystals, gray/green, pale green, blue, colorless, or gray/white in color. The brilliant flashes of blue, red, gold, and green are due to light interference within the structure of the minerals' composition.
BRINGS: magic
CHAKRA: crown
HEALING FOCUS: aura
CRYSTAL GRID KEYWORDS: magic, aura, stability, flow of energy, chakra, right/left brain activity, magic and science, intuition and intellect, mental sharpness, inspiration, originality, possibilities, security, calm, confidence, peace.

Below: Opal ignites the fires of creativity and passion.

MULTICOLORED

TOURMALINE

Vertically striated prismatic crystals in most colors—green (verdelite), blue (indicolite), pink (elbaite), red (rubellite), yellow (tsilasite), black (schorl), brown (dravite), green or blue with pink center (watermelon), or colors reversed, bi-colors, tri-colors, lime green often with white center, colorless (achroite), and lavender.
COLORS THAT APPEAR IN THIS BOOK: green, pink, black, watermelon, and blue.
BRINGS: protection
CHAKRA: all, depending on variety
HEALING FOCUS: mind
CRYSTAL GRID KEYWORDS: balance, calming, new challenges, confidence, unblocking, openness, freedom, positivity, negotiation, skill, talent, carefree, detox, protection, inspiration, self-confidence, yin/yang, aura, awareness, psychic ability, healing ability, connection, left/right brain, groups, creativity, inner self, laughter, joy, happiness.

FLUORITE

Cubic, octahedral, and rhombododecahedral crystals and masses. Colors include purple, clear, blue, green, yellow, brown, pink, red, black, and rainbow. Rainbow fluorite may include green, purple, blue, and clear/colorless bands in the same specimen. Fluorite is also known as fluor spar.
COLORS THAT APPEAR IN THIS BOOK: yellow, rainbow, green, and blue.
BRINGS: focus, order out of chaos
CHAKRA: brow
HEALING FOCUS: infections
CRYSTAL GRID KEYWORDS: structure, calming, focus, organization, de-stress, decisions, concentration, relationships, groups, meditation, detox, carers, weight management, technology.

CALCITE

Masses, stalactites, scalenohedral, and rhombohedral crystals. Common colors include green, blue, yellow, golden, orange, clear (Iceland spa), white, brown, pink, red, black, gray and pink (cobaltoan calcite).
COLORS THAT APPEAR IN THIS BOOK: red, orange, golden, green, blue, white, Iceland spa, and cobaltoan.
BRINGS: balance
CHAKRA: all, specific to variety
HEALING FOCUS: emotions
CRYSTAL GRID KEYWORDS: balance, emotions, calming, confidence, stress, yin/yang, a feel-better stone, travel, channeling, teaching, studying, learning, art, science, seeing the bigger picture, growth.

Right: Tourmaline crystals stand guard, protecting your energy from unhealthy and negative drains and influences.

BLUE

DUMORTIERITE
Blue and pink/brown masses.
BRINGS: understanding of the cause
of dis-ease
CHAKRA: brow
HEALING FOCUS: ligaments
CRYSTAL GRID KEYWORDS: hidden
inspiration, excitability, stubbornness,
solidity, quiet confidence, stamina,
patience, communication, expression,
helps you to speak your mind.

TURQUOISE
Blue, green, or blue/green masses,
crusts, and, rarely, small, short,
prismatic crystals.
BRINGS: clarity to see your own path
and walk it
CHAKRA: throat
HEALING FOCUS: allergies
CRYSTAL GRID KEYWORDS:
multipurpose healer, structure, throat,
communication, public speaking, creative
expression, courage, emotional balance,
friendship, regeneration, love, travel,
protection for travelers, detox,
meditation, spirit contact, astral travel,
spirituality, peace of mind, protection
of property, protection from accidents,
yin/yang, writing, psychic ability,
wisdom, seeing the beauty in everything,
open-mindedness, compassion, romance,
positivity, recovery.

AZURITE
Masses, nodules, and, rarely, tabular
and prismatic crystals of azure or
paler blues.
BRINGS: thoughts and psychic
information
CHAKRA: throat
HEALING FOCUS: nervous system
CRYSTAL GRID KEYWORDS:
creativity, inspiration, imagination,
psychic ability, expression, compassion,
empathy, selflessness, art, music,
performance.

ANGELITE
Blue/white nodules, masses, and
occasionally crystals.
BRINGS: connection
CHAKRA: throat
HEALING FOCUS: psychic and
spiritual healing
CRYSTAL GRID KEYWORDS: feeling
of security, comfort, grief, awareness,
communication, spirit guides, channeling,
telepathy, connection, angels, guardians,
totem animals, balance, protection,
astral travel, numbers, peacefulness,
serenity, calmness, rebirthing, senses.

AQUAMARINE
Blue/green variety of beryl, forming
hexagonal prismatic crystals with flat
or occasionally small pyramidal
terminations.
BRINGS: protection for travelers
CHAKRA: throat
HEALING FOCUS: body fluids
CRYSTAL GRID KEYWORDS:
protection, travel, calming, gentle,
cooling, communication, courage,
intellect, study, learning, pollutants, flow
(making things happen), washing away
blocks, spiritual awareness, spiritual
development, centering, truth about
yourself, self-awareness, inner self, higher
self, compassion, acceptance, meditation,
responsibility, tolerance, vision.

BLUE CHALCEDONY
Light blue variety of chalcedony.
BRINGS: emotional expression
CHAKRA: throat
HEALING FOCUS: childhood issues
CRYSTAL GRID KEYWORDS: release,
letting go, past, communication,
expression, forgiveness.

LARIMAR

Massive variety of pectolite often found in radial groupings. Colors include blue, green, gray, and red, all possibly with white.
BRINGS: soft gentle healing energy
CHAKRA: heart
HEALING FOCUS: addiction to the material world
CRYSTAL GRID KEYWORDS: soothing, freedom, peacefulness, expression, Earth healing, seeing who you really are, inner self, confidence, acceptance.

KYANITE

Blade-type crystals, fibers, and masses. Colors include blue, black, gray, white, green, yellow, and pink.
BRINGS: help in speaking for yourself with confidence
CHAKRA: throat
HEALING FOCUS: chakra alignment
CRYSTAL GRID KEYWORDS: voice, expression, communication, throat, singing voice, tranquility, calm, perseverance, reason, meditation, connection, spirit guides, dream recall, dream understanding, yin/yang, attunement, sacred ceremony, psychic ability, awareness, stamina, endurance, flow.

BLUE QUARTZ

Clear or white quartz with blue tourmaline (indicolite) inclusions. **Note:** several other minerals are also called "blue quartz," such as sodalite, siderite, dumortierite, blue quartz (China). This entry does not refer to them.
BRINGS: bliss
CHAKRA: throat
HEALING FOCUS: metabolism
CRYSTAL GRID KEYWORDS: connection, the universe, spirit guides, communication, expression, clear mind, release, grounding, energy shift, well-being, emotional balance, happiness, calmness, peacefulness, introversion, belief, confidence, trust, self-reliance, spontaneity, contentment, happiness, joy, vitality, awareness, telepathy, insight, truth.

SAPPHIRE

Gem variety of corundum found in any color except red (which is ruby)—typically blue, but also yellow, green, black, purple, pink, and white.
BRINGS: fulfillment of ambition
CHAKRA: brow
HEALING FOCUS: glands
CRYSTAL GRID KEYWORDS: dreams, goals, emotional balance, desire, wisdom, youthfulness, structure, connection, spirit guides, seeing the beauty in everything, comfort, contentment, open-mindedness, happiness, joy, fun, intuition, ancestors, akashic records, astral travel.

SODALITE

Blue or blue and white masses, nodules, and, rarely, dodecahedral and hexagonal prismatic crystals. Other colors include gray, green, yellow, white, red, and colorless.
BRINGS: self-esteem
CHAKRA: brow
HEALING FOCUS: lymphatic system
CRYSTAL GRID KEYWORDS: calming, balance, creative expression, endurance, confidence, strength, sleep, sensitivity, perception, youthfulness, babies, composure, organization, self-confidence, self-esteem, communication of feelings, ideas, groups.

TANZANITE

Variety of zoisite, forming masses and prismatic, striated crystals, typically blue. Other colors include yellow, gray/blue, and purple.
BRINGS: results
CHAKRA: throat, brow, crown
HEALING FOCUS: eyes
CRYSTAL GRID KEYWORDS: communication, psychic ability, spirit guides, meditation, visualization, magic, stamina, inner strength, vitality, positivity.

LAPIS LAZULI
Massive rock, cubic, and dodecahedral crystals; very often includes lazurite, calcite, and pyrite.
BRINGS: dreams
CHAKRA: brow
HEALING FOCUS: skeleton, bones
CRYSTAL GRID KEYWORDS:
structure, creative expression, happiness, pleasure, peace, relaxation, vitality, wisdom, psychic ability, natural gifts, talent, skill, dreams, visions, endurance, stamina, detox, organization, yin/yang, relationships, a feel-better stone, sleep, balance.

AQUA AURA
Quartz crystal bonded with gold giving beautiful, mostly clear, blue crystals and clusters.
BRINGS: positivity
CHAKRA: brow, throat
HEALING FOCUS: trauma
CRYSTAL GRID KEYWORDS: aura, communication, protection, psychic ability, positivity, confidence, happiness, loss, grief, a feel-better stone, contentment, recovery, comfort, discovery.

BLUE LACE AGATE
Pale blue and white banded variety of agate.
BRINGS: calmness
CHAKRA: throat
HEALING FOCUS: throat—speaking your truth
CRYSTAL GRID KEYWORDS:
communication, gentle, calming, balance, emotions, eyesight, speech, spirituality, spiritual ideas, attunement, honesty, expression.

VIOLET

CHAROITE
Massive sometimes with inclusions of white quartz and black manganese.
BRINGS: your spiritual experiences into your physical world
CHAKRA: crown
HEALING FOCUS: learning disorders
CRYSTAL GRID KEYWORDS: breaking cycles, analysis, releasing old relationships, attention span, being in the moment, opportunities, meditation, clairvoyance, intuition, moving forward, detox.

LEPIDOLITE
Masses, layered plates ("books"), short prismatic and tabular crystals in a variety of colors including lavender (pink to purple), yellow, gray, colorless, and white.
BRINGS: learning
CHAKRA: heart and brow
HEALING FOCUS: stress-related conditions
CRYSTAL GRID KEYWORDS: study, knowledge, ideas, awareness, stress, contentedness, joy, happiness, transition, death, change, addictive personalities, astral travel, birth, rebirth, trust, calming, abundance, youthfulness, confidence.

AMETRINE
Mixture of amethyst and citrine, purple and gold in color.
BRINGS: intellectual understanding of spirituality
CHAKRA: solar plexus and crown
HEALING FOCUS: physical, mental, emotional, and spiritual blockages
CRYSTAL GRID KEYWORDS:
yin/yang, inspiration, creativity, meditation, peacefulness, tranquility, aura, relaxation, tolerance, understanding, open-mindedness, astral travel, change.

SPIRIT QUARTZ

Purple (amethyst) or white (quartz), sometimes with orange/brown iron inclusions or surface staining.
BRINGS: sense of belonging
CHAKRA: crown
HEALING FOCUS: your dark side
CRYSTAL GRID KEYWORDS: sociable, groups, work environments, sports, teams, team building, grief, fertility, abundance, release of emotions, revitalizing, astral travel, dreams, protection, patience, self-esteem, past experiences, past lives, rebirthing, fear of success, psychic ability, inner self, higher self, flow, behavior patterns, detox, meditation, enchantment.

SUGILITE

Violet masses and, rarely, tiny crystals.
BRINGS: mind-body link in disease—helpful in the treatment of most illnesses
CHAKRA: crown
HEALING FOCUS: holistic, whole body healing
CRYSTAL GRID KEYWORDS: balance, confidence, courage, challenges, children, spiritual love, spirit contact, life path, mission, forgiveness, eccentricity, friendship, kindness, softness, joy, happiness, peacefulness, calmness, contentment, open-mindedness, pleasure, cheer, uplifting, creativity.

SUPER SEVEN

Comprises seven different minerals: amethyst, cacoxenite, goethite, lepidocrocite, quartz, rutile, and smoky quartz. Super seven is found in just one location, in Brazil. Small segments of the mineral exhibit all the healing qualities even though all seven minerals may not be present in the specimen. The energy of the original mass seems to give super seven its wonderful healing potential. Super seven is also known as sacred seven and melody stone.
BRINGS: advancement and fulfillment of dreams, goals, and ideals
CHAKRA: all
HEALING FOCUS: karma
CRYSTAL GRID KEYWORDS: aura, connection, spirit guides, awareness, psychic ability, truth, spiritual connection, love, relationships, reincarnation, past lives, peace, harmony, creativity, Earth healing.

PURPLE RAY OPAL /VIOLET FLAME OPAL

Naturally occurring massive mixture of common white and purple opal.
BRINGS: release from blocks you create
CHAKRA: crown, heart
HEALING FOCUS: past, past lives
CRYSTAL GRID KEYWORDS: connection, ceremony, angels, spirit guides, tranquility, serenity, soothing, calming, emotion, awareness, psychic ability, cleansing, inner strength, courage, love, peace, harmony.

AMETHYST

Variety of quartz found as crystals or masses. Its classic purple color is due to manganese and iron inclusions. Amethyst may also be almost black (rare), purple and white banded (chevron amethyst, also known as banded amethyst), and green, which is colored by mineral inclusions (prasiolite).
BRINGS: forward movement in life
CHAKRA: crown
HEALING FOCUS: blood infection, head
CRYSTAL GRID KEYWORDS: behavior patterns, peacefulness, calmness, cleansing, detox, clearing, faithfulness, chastity, calm passion, emotional energy, grief, homesickness, sleep, confidence, relaxation, negotiation skills, sensitivity, purification for ceremonies, meditation, connection to reiki, spirituality, spirit contact, balance, aura, protection, responsibility, decisions, wealth, business success, temperament, flow, change, healing the cause of dis-ease, public speaking, listening, posture, self-esteem, survival instinct.

HERKIMER DIAMOND

Clear, stubby, double-terminated quartz crystal. The only place it's found is Herkimer County, New York State, USA. (Other diamond-style quartz crystals come from Pakistan, Mexico, Romania, and Tunisia. These are not the same and, although they may be wonderful crystals in themselves, they are not covered in this entry.)
BRINGS: power to overcome
CHAKRA: crown
HEALING FOCUS: DNA genetic healing
CRYSTAL GRID KEYWORDS: stress, cleansing, spontaneity, being in the moment, courage, relaxation, new beginnings, attunements, energy, people, connection, psychic ability, memory, detox, softness, calmness.

HOWLITE

White and off-white nodules, masses, and, rarely, crystals; often dyed and used to imitate more expensive stones.
BRINGS: discernment
CHAKRA: crown
HEALING FOCUS: immune system
CRYSTAL GRID KEYWORDS: calm communication, memory, action, goals, selflessness, stress, kindness, boisterousness, emotional expression, memory, study, learning, vulgarity.

ANGEL AURA QUARTZ

Quartz crystal bonded with platinum and silver.
BRINGS: empathy
CHAKRA: all
HEALING FOCUS: karma
CRYSTAL GRID KEYWORDS: connection, angels, aura, protection, akashic records, nurture, caring professions, love, peace, harmony.

CRYOLITE

Massive white to off-white translucent mineral.
BRINGS: direction to your spiritual journey
CHAKRA: crown and heart
HEALING FOCUS: brain
CRYSTAL GRID KEYWORDS: decisions, spirit guides, angels, enlightenment, connection, growth, potential, emotion, release, spiritual path, goals, focus, awareness, love, energy, calming, public speaking.

PETALITE

Masses in clear, white, pink, gray, green/white, and red/white.
BRINGS: the courage of your convictions; encourages you to walk your walk
CHAKRA: crown
HEALING FOCUS: effects of cancer
CRYSTAL GRID KEYWORDS: spirituality, connection, angels, spirit guides, totem animals, shamanic visions, astral travel, peace of mind, meditation, agility, dexterity, flexibility, aura, psychic ability, yin/yang.

PHENACITE

Colorless (may be tinted) rhombohedral and slender prismatic crystals, masses, and fibrous spherical structures.
BRINGS: healing on many levels
CHAKRA: crown and brow
HEALING FOCUS: mental health
CRYSTAL GRID KEYWORDS: awareness, meditation, energy, cleansing, focus, peacefulness, calming.

RUTILATED QUARTZ

Quartz with silver, golden, or black threads of rutile.
BRINGS: regeneration
CHAKRA: brow and crown
HEALING FOCUS: depression
CRYSTAL GRID KEYWORDS: calmness, balance, happiness, joy, vitality, strength, activity, positivity, youthfulness, purpose.

QUARTZ CRYSTAL

Hexagonal crystals and masses, clear or white, sometimes with inclusions. Quartz is the most abundant mineral on the earth's surface. Over 70 percent of the land we walk on is formed from quartz in one form or another. Quartz crystals are relatively rare and clear quartz crystals very rare.
BRINGS: focus
CHAKRA: all
HEALING FOCUS: channeling all energies, so helps with any condition
CRYSTAL GRID KEYWORDS: relief, energy, balance, meditation, focusing, positivity, structure, routine, organization, weight loss, a feel-better stone, quality of life, happiness, energizing, zest for life, all-singing all-dancing, joy, healing, self-esteem, confidence, clarity.

TOURMALINATED QUARTZ

Quartz with black tourmaline rods growing through it.
BRINGS: answers
CHAKRA: all
HEALING FOCUS: nervous system
CRYSTAL GRID KEYWORDS: childhood, experiences, behavior patterns, happiness, joy, zest, confidence, inner strength, problem-solving, discovery, adventure, inner self, self-awareness.

MOONSTONE

Variety of feldspar exhibiting chatoyancy. Colors include white, cream, black, yellow, brown, blue, green (parrot), and rainbow (white with blue color flash).
BRINGS: a caring attitude
CHAKRA: sacral
HEALING FOCUS: women's health
CRYSTAL GRID KEYWORDS: calming, emotions, emotional energy, release of blocks, control, balance, compassion, oversensitivity, soothing, fertility, pregnancy, childbirth, femininity, sexuality, passion, peace of mind, wisdom, inner self, cycles, repeated patterns, change, new beginnings, endings, optimism, intuition, insight, creativity, confidence, composure, protection for travelers, good luck, happy home, youthfulness.

SELENITE

Crystallized form of gypsum, usually clear or white.
BRINGS: natural cycles
CHAKRA: crown
HEALING FOCUS: skin conditions
CRYSTAL GRID KEYWORDS: sensitivity, fertility, sex drive, kindness, willingness, helpfulness, structure, youthfulness, light, longevity, cycles, patterns.

MAGNESITE

Masses and nodules that look a bit like 200-million-year-old chewing gum! Usually white, but also gray, brown, and yellow. Rarely forms rhombohedral, prismatic, tabular, and scalenohedral crystals.
BRINGS: passion
CHAKRA: crown
HEALING FOCUS: balances body temperature
CRYSTAL GRID KEYWORDS: intellect, meditation, visualization, love, detox, boiling pot of ideas, collaboration, teams, colleagues, friendship, relationships.

Lodestone Magnetite

LODESTONE/MAGNETITE

Magnetic black/brown masses and octahedral crystals. Magnetite is the same mineral without the magnetism, forming black or brown octahedral crystals, masses, and dendrites. Where there is a magnetic polarity in the specimen it is known as lodestone.
BRINGS: grounding
CHAKRA: base
HEALING FOCUS: muscles, bones, back
CRYSTAL GRID KEYWORDS: receptivity, attraction, attachment, magnetism, acceptance, getting the best from uncomfortable situations, being in the moment, energy flow, yin/yang, letting go of burdens ("like taking a weight off my shoulders"), security, independence, clarity, seeing "signposts," grief, confidence, calmness, peacefulness, wealth, satisfaction, meditation, protection (especially for healers and those in the caring professions who need protecting from clients' energy and empathic symptoms), tenacity, endurance, remote viewing, attracting love, desires, trust, intuition.

BLACK OBSIDIAN

Black volcanic glass.
BRINGS: spirituality into your everyday life
CHAKRA: base
HEALING FOCUS: digestive system
CRYSTAL GRID KEYWORDS: grounding, protection, amalgamation, integration, sexuality, male energies, masculinity, survival instinct, connection, shamanism, creativity, intuition, past, new beginnings, inner self, mirror of the soul.

APACHE TEAR

Translucent black or brown volcanic glass nodules.
BRINGS: release of suppressed tears and emotions
CHAKRA: base
HEALING FOCUS: grief and loss
CRYSTAL GRID KEYWORDS: change, emotional balance, forgiveness, positivity, moving forward in life, spontaneity, self-limiting, detox, connection, Earth healing.

SNOWFLAKE OBSIDIAN

Black obsidian with inclusions of white phenocryst.
BRINGS: release of anger and resentment
CHAKRA: base
HEALING FOCUS: stomach and sinuses—the meridian linking these two areas (ties in with the tradition that kids with runny tummies have runny noses)
CRYSTAL GRID KEYWORDS: vision, peace of mind, release, new beginnings, loneliness, meditation, purity, grounding, survival skills, direction.

TEKTITE

Meteoritic glass created from the immense heat of a meteorite impact with the earth. The heat is so intense that both the meteorite and the earth's surface melt. Tektite is formed as this mixture of space material and earth cool together. Colors are black, brown, yellow (Libyan glass), and green (moldavite).
BRINGS: contact with new possibilities and worlds
CHAKRA: crown
HEALING FOCUS: circulation
CRYSTAL GRID KEYWORDS: yin/yang, fertility, abundance, reasoning, passion, psychic ability, meditation, distant healing, Earth healing.

BLACK MOONSTONE

Black variety of feldspar exhibiting chatoyancy.
BRINGS: access to positive use of your dark side's energies
CHAKRA: base
HEALING FOCUS: hormones
CRYSTAL GRID KEYWORDS: children, organized, abundance, new beginnings, growth, release, emotion, security, grounding, concentration, focus, relationships, love, romance, loyalty, business, inspiration, intuition, aura, new moon energy, calming.

JET

Fossilized remains of trees.
BRINGS: sexual energy
CHAKRA: base
HEALING FOCUS: stomach
CRYSTAL GRID KEYWORDS: yin/yang, protection, happiness, joy, confidence, power, inner strength, wealth, business success, energy with calmness.

RAINBOW OBSIDIAN

Black volcanic glass exhibiting color chatoyancy from light reflecting off bubbles inside the stone.
BRINGS: connection to nature
CHAKRA: base
HEALING FOCUS: emotional wounds
CRYSTAL GRID KEYWORDS: love, seeing the beauty in everything, connection, inner self, divination, happiness, positivity, generosity, stress, aura, hypnosis.

BLACK BANDED AGATE

Variety of agate showing black and white banding.
BRINGS: answers by seeing things differently
CHAKRA: base
HEALING FOCUS: emotions
CRYSTAL GRID KEYWORDS: yin/yang, endurance, death, change, new beginnings, start, mystery, hidden depths, protection.

Above: Black stones are generally grounding for any situation, helping to bring it into reality.

GRAY/SILVER

PYRITE

Cubic and dodecahedral crystals, occasionally flattened (pyrite suns), and masses. Pyrite becomes more golden with oxidation and may replace other minerals, so can be found in many formations and shapes as pseudomorphs and in combination with other minerals. It's also known as fool's gold and iron pyrites.

BRINGS: a place of silence within you
CHAKRA: all, especially solar plexus
HEALING FOCUS: circulation
CRYSTAL GRID KEYWORDS: energy sparks, creativity, leadership, positivity, memory, past, thought processes, protection, protection from accidents, cleansing, new beginnings, fresh start, ideas, creation, possibility.

GRAY BANDED AGATE

Gray and white banded or patterned variety of agate.
BRINGS: useable store of energy
CHAKRA: sacral
HEALING FOCUS: fatigue, general malaise, ME
CRYSTAL GRID KEYWORDS: protection, power, direction, pliability, flexibility, vision, clarity, sexual energy, relationships, faithfulness, talent, skill, ability.

HEMATITE

Metallic gray/silver when polished; black and brick red/brown masses, botryoidal forms, rosettes, layered plates, and tabular and rhombohedral crystals.
BRINGS: grounding
CHAKRA: base
HEALING FOCUS: blood disorders
CRYSTAL GRID KEYWORDS: courage, strength, grounding, personal magnetism, stress, travel, sleep, mental processes, thoughts, memory, dexterity, numbers/maths, yin/yang, positivity, attracts love, meditation.

STIBNITE

Columns, blades, needle-like and prismatic crystals with obvious vertical striations, and masses.
BRINGS: the ability to find your path in life
CHAKRA: crown
HEALING FOCUS: throat and esophagus
CRYSTAL GRID KEYWORDS: direction, choices, decisions, teaching, communication, meditation, protection, money, relationships, attractiveness, totem animals, connection with the wolf, teacher, path finder, loyalty in relationships, speed, endurance, flexibility.

BROWN

CRAZY LACE AGATE

Variety of agate with "crazy" patterns, bands, and wavy lines of cream, red, and brown. It's also known as Mexican lace agate.
BRINGS: confidence
CHAKRA: heart
HEALING FOCUS: speech, communication
CRYSTAL GRID KEYWORDS: confidence, inner strength, balance, courage, self-esteem, vitality, communication.

TURRITELLA AGATE

Massive brown agate with fossil inclusions.
BRINGS: a balanced perspective
CHAKRA: base
HEALING FOCUS: digestion, peristalsis, stomach upsets, absorption of food, bloating, wind pains
CRYSTAL GRID KEYWORDS: middle path, positivity, change, survival instinct, time, renewal, Earth healing.

ARAGONITE

Hexagonal column-shaped crystals, often linked, twinned, and interpenetrating, forming "sputniks." It can also form fibers, masses, and stalactites. Colors are white, brown, yellow, blue, or green.
BRINGS: clarity—answers suddenly become obvious
CHAKRA: crown
HEALING FOCUS: stress-related conditions, such as eczema and psoriasis
CRYSTAL GRID KEYWORDS: stress, calmness, peacefulness, meditation, problem-solving, patience, practicality, reliability, youthfulness.

MUSCOVITE

Variety of mica usually forming layered plates, flowers, "books," scales, and masses and other crystalline forms. Colors include brown, green, pink, gray, violet, yellow, red, and white.
BRINGS: security
CHAKRA: heart
HEALING FOCUS: releasing painful emotions
CRYSTAL GRID KEYWORDS: self-confidence, optimism, past, calmness, forgiveness, peacefulness, energy, speed of thought, expression, intuition, problem-solving, major life decisions, higher self, shamanic visions, meditation, sleep, dreams, knowledge, understanding, learning.

SMOKY QUARTZ

Brown or black variety of quartz colored by natural radiation from the earth.
BRINGS: speed to the laws of karma
CHAKRA: base
HEALING FOCUS: depression, despair, grief
CRYSTAL GRID KEYWORDS: dreams, understanding, vitality, expression, sexual energy, mental activity, positivity, relaxation, voice, peacefulness, calmness, grounding, moving forward in life, new beginnings, energy healing, channeling energy, protection, ceremony, ritual, meditation, male energies, survival instincts, intuition, self-discipline.

Above: Intent that is focused through a crystal grid is a very powerful tool. When you create a crystal grid with your clear and focused energy, mind and thoughts, you are telling the universe what you would like it to do.

PETRIFIED WOOD

Fossilized trees in which organic material has been replaced by one or more minerals, usually agate, chalcedony, and quartz, but many other types can be present. Colors include brown, but can be any wood-like color, or agate, chalcedony, and opal colors.
BRINGS: comfort
CHAKRA: base
HEALING FOCUS: bones
CRYSTAL GRID KEYWORDS: balance, soothing, grounding, longevity, freshness, stress, childhood, past, past lives, innocence, structure, solidity, framework, strength.

SEPTARIAN

Nodules of clay ironstone into which other minerals, such as calcite, jasper, dolomite, aragonite, and, occasionally, barite, are deposited through small cracks in the structure. Other minerals may also be present.
BRINGS: confidence
CHAKRA: base
HEALING FOCUS: bones and muscles
CRYSTAL GRID KEYWORDS: public speaking, communication, art, music, voice, patience, endurance, tolerance, understanding, awareness, environment, flexibility, Earth healing.

SACRED GEOMETRY

In this section you will find all the grids used in Chapter 4. For simpler grids, you can place your crystals directly onto the page, trace the grid, or photocopy the grid. For more complex grids, it is best to enlarge the grids on a photocopier, printing them on tabloid-size (A3) paper. The grids are also available to download from www.thecrystalhealer.co.uk.

CIRCLE

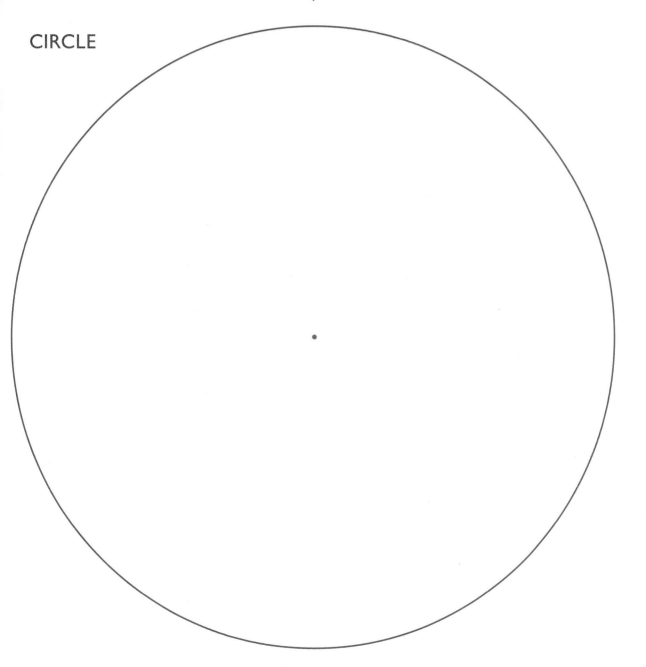

Distant healing, page 92

CRYSTAL CHAKRA GRID

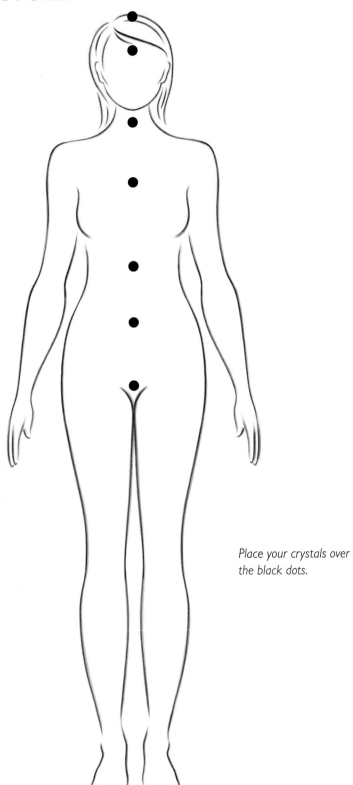

Place your crystals over the black dots.

TRIANGLE

Mental power, page 114

DOUBLE TRIANGLE

Strength and physical ability, page 117

CONCENTRIC CIRCLES

Meditation focus, page 86

HEXAGON

An energizing crystal grid, page 36

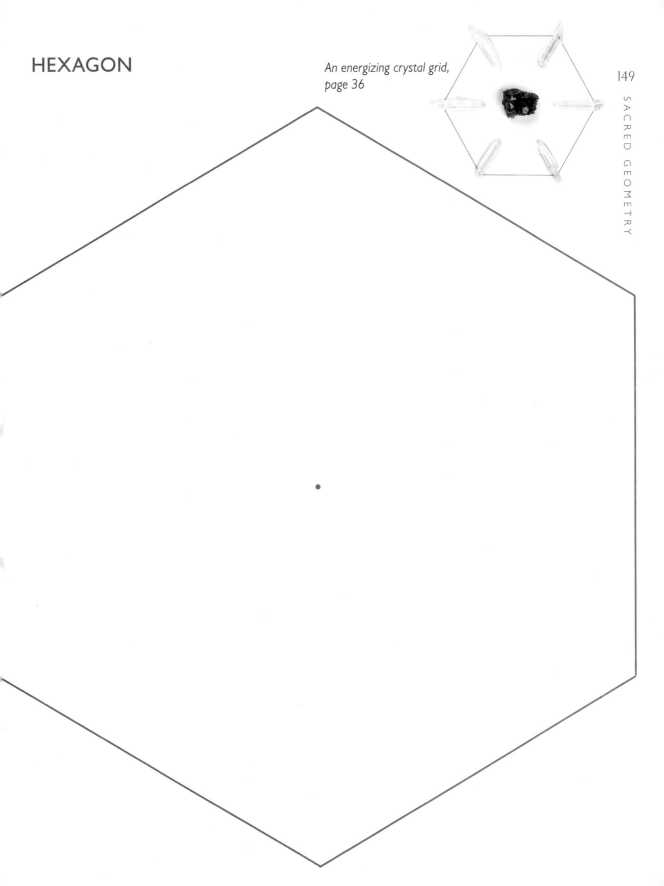

SQUARE

To use for the Sports grid on page 118, turn the
grid by 45° so the points of the square are set
to north, south, east, and west.

Creativity, page 52

INTERLOCKING SQUARES

Communication, page 70

Self-love, page 99

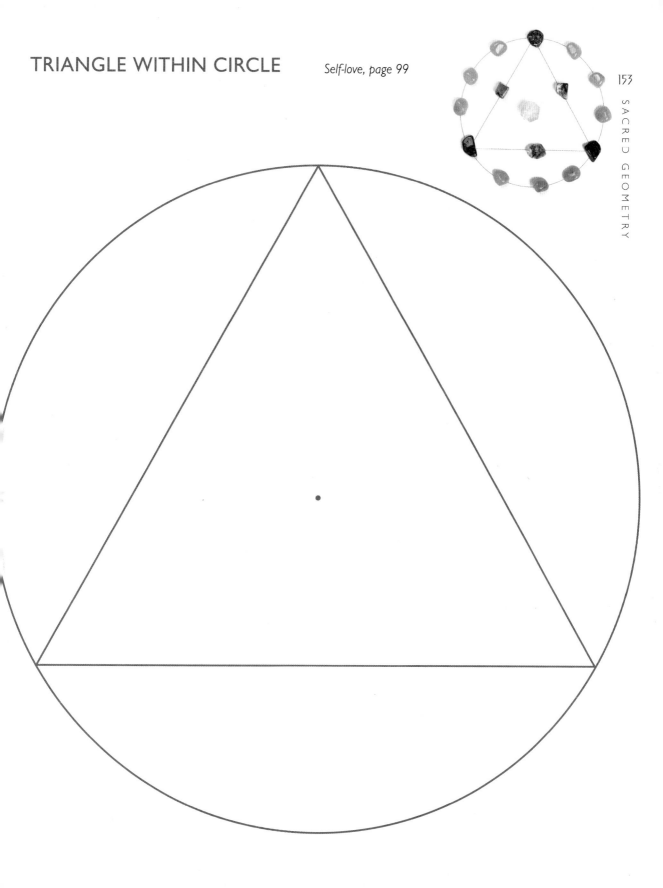

FLOWER OF LIFE

Abundance, page 50

METATRON'S CUBE

Health and healing, page 119

GLOSSARY

AGGREGATE A mixture of minerals combined in a geological process; resembles a solid rock.

AKASHIC RECORDS A library of spiritual information that exists on another plane.

ALLUVIAL Made from sediment in riverbeds which produces "river-tumbled" crystals.

ASTRAL TRAVEL The ability to send a part of the astral/spirit body to travel outside of the physical body (while remaining connected to the physical body).

AURA The subtle energy field (qv) around the body.

BLADE A crystal that resembles a flat knife blade.

BOTRYOIDAL Describes bulbous minerals that resemble a bunch of grapes.

CHAKRA The Sanskrit word for "wheel." Chakras are the energy centers of the body, appearing as wheels to people who see energy.

CHANNELING The communication of messages or information from the spirit world via a medium.

CHATOYANCY An optical effect, also known as "cat's eye," found in some polished crystals. Chatoyant crystals bring good luck, happiness, and serenity. They raise intuition and awareness, provide protection, and can help with disorders of the eyes, night vision, and headaches. The astrological associations of

these crystals are Capricorn, Taurus, and Aries.

CHI In Chinese medicine and philosophy, chi is the energy or life force of the universe, believed to flow around the body and to be present in all living things. Other cultures call chi by different names, such as prana in India.

CLAIRAUDIENCE The ability to hear psychic information.

CLAIRVOYANCE The ability to see psychic information.

CRUST The top or outer layer. Crystals occurring as crusts are growing on the surface of a rock or mineral. *See also* DRUSE.

CUBIC Describes a cube-shaped crystal, with six square faces. The three axes are the same length and are at right angles to one another.

DENDRITE A mineral that crystallizes in the shape of a tree or branch or grows through another crystal or rock, creating the impression of a tree or branches.

DIS-EASE A state of unsoundness on any level (physical, emotional, mental, or spiritual), which may weaken the body's natural defense systems and increase the risk of illness or disease. It relates to underlying causes and not a specific illness or disease.

DISTANT HEALING The process of sending healing energy, good thoughts, or prayers to a person who is not present—perhaps

someone in another country. Also known as absent healing or remote healing.

DODECAHEDRAL Describes a crystal having 12 pentagonal (five-sided) faces meeting in threes at 20 vertexes.

DRUSE A surface crust of small crystals on a rock of the same or a different mineral.

ENERGY A supply or source of power: electrical, nuclear, mechanical, or subtle (qv), such as chi (qv).

FELDSPAR A group of silicate minerals.

GEODE A hollow rock with crystals growing in the cavity.

HEXAGONAL Describes a crystal system having four axes, of which the three horizontal axes are equal in length and cross at 120° angles, and the vertical axis is a different length and at right angles to the others. A hexagonal crystal has eight faces.

INCLUSION A mineral found within the structure of a different mineral.

IRIDESCENCE Colors appearing inside a crystal owing to either diffraction or refraction of light within the crystalline structure.

MASS Matter that has no definable crystalline structure.

MERIDIAN An energy pathway through the body. Meridians carry chi in the same way that veins and arteries carry blood.

NODULE A form of a mineral that is massive (see MASS) with a rounded outer surface.

OCTAHEDRAL Describes a crystal having eight faces that are all equilateral triangles; resembles two four-sided pyramids joined at the bases.

PLAGIOCLASE A series of feldspars, including labradorite and sunstone.

PLATE A crystal that has grown flattened and often thin.

PRISMATIC Describes a crystal having faces that are similar in size and shape and that run parallel to an axis; the ends are rectilinear and similar in size and shape. For example, a triangular prismatic crystal has two triangular ends joined by three rectangular faces, while a hexagonal prismatic crystal has two hexagonal ends connected by six rectangular faces.

PSEUDOMORPH A mineral that replaces another within the original's crystal structure. As a result, the new mineral has the external shape of the departed one.

PSYCHIC ABILITIES These include intuition or gut feelings, channeling (qv), clairaudience (qv), clairvoyance (qv), sensing energies and auras (qv), seeing auras, interpreting auras, telepathy, extrasensory perception, and increased insight into divination and tarot card readings.

PYRAMIDAL Describes a crystal in which the base is a polygon (i.e. with at least three straight sides) and the other faces are triangles that meet at a point.

REIKI A form of hands-on healing that originated in Japan and now has millions of practitioners worldwide.

REMOTE HEALING See DISTANT HEALING.

REMOTE VIEWING The ability to see places and events at a distance. See also ASTRAL TRAVEL.

RHOMBIC Describes crystals with a parallelogram shape (a parallelogram has four equal sides and oblique angles).

RHOMBODODECAHEDRAL Describes crystals that have 12 equal sides with oblique angles.

RHOMBOHEDRAL Describes crystals having six faces, each of them a rhombus (which has four equal sides, with opposite sides parallel, and no right angles). A rhombohedron resembles a cube that is skewed to one side.

SCALENOHEDRAL Describes crystals having 12 faces, each of them a scalene triangle (which has three unequal sides).

SHAMANIC HEALING An umbrella term covering a multitude of ancient forms of healing, all of which are linked to nature. One of the oldest forms of traditional healing.

SPHENOID Wedge-shaped.

SPIRIT GUIDES The beings or energies of departed souls who impart information, knowledge, and wisdom to help you on your path.

STRIATED Describes crystals having parallel grooves or markings along their length.

SUBTLE ENERGY Energy that is outside of the known electromagnetic spectrum and therefore not easily detected.

TABULAR Describes crystals that are broad and flat.

TEKTITE Small glassy rock formed from meteorite impact.

TETRAHEDRAL Describes crystals having four triangular faces.

TOTEM ANIMALS Animal spirits or characteristics that help to guide you on your path in life.

TRAPEZOHEDRAL Describes crystals having faces that each have four non-parallel sides (a shape known as a trapezium in the US and a trapezoid in the UK).

INDEX

NOTES

1. (p. 6) F. Sicher and E. Targ et al, "A randomized double-blind study of the effect of distant healing in a population with advanced AIDS: report of a small-scale study", *Western Journal of Medicine*, 1998; 168(6): 356–63.
2. (p. 7) "Quantum Theory Demonstrated: Observation Affects Reality", February 27, 1998, Weizmann Institute of Science; Prof. Mordehai Heiblum, PhD student Eyal Buks, Dr Ralph Schuster, Dr Diana Mahalu, and Dr Vladimir Umansky of the Condensed Matter Physics Department at the Institute's Joseph H. and Belle R. Braun Center for Submicron Research.
3. (p. 11) Margo McCaffery is an American registered nurse and pioneer in the field of pain management nursing.

ACKNOWLEDGMENTS

The support from my wife is an essential part of writing a book. So, I would like to thank my wonderful wife Lyn Palmer for her love, input, and support; for reading through pages and pages at different stages, suggesting ideas and edits, and her experience, expertise, and patience.

Also, my clients and students, who provide a wealth of experience for me to share with you. All the people at CICO Books for their input: Carmel Edmonds, Sally Powell, Yvonne Doolan, Kerry Lewis, Anna Galkina, and particularly Cindy Richards for the good sense to publish this book. Finally, but perhaps most importantly, the people who inspired me to write: my father Cyril, American crystal healer Melody, and Ian, who knows why.

My sincere thanks to every other crystal author, whether I've read their books or not, for helping to spread the crystal word, as well as to everyone inspired to improve, change, or heal themselves or others by reading this book.